W9-CGO-611

ISBN 0-9693049-0-0

Produced and Published by:
The Blue Flame Kitchen
Canadian Western Natural Gas
909 11th Avenue S.W.
Calgary, Alberta T2R 1L8
(403) 245-7731

Design and Art:
A. Hordos Designs Ltd.
Calgary, Alberta

Photography:
Belinda Grootveld and John Salus
Calgary, Alberta

China, silver and other
accessories:
Marcel de Paris
Calgary, Alberta

Typesetting and
Colour Separations:
Colour Four Graphic Services
Calgary, Alberta

Printed and bound in Canada by:
Ronalds Printing
Calgary, Alberta

Co-ordinated by:
Public Relations Department
Canadian Western Natural Gas

Introduction

The Blue Flame Kitchen's barbecuing, bread-making and Christmas entertaining programs are well-known and widely appreciated. It is from these demonstrations that the majority of the following "75 Favorites" have been selected.

The recipes were originally drawn from our extensive reference library and outstanding recipes sent to us by our customers. They were made repeatedly in our test kitchen at the Canadian Western Centre in Calgary, and developed where necessary for high altitude (more than 3,000 feet). The recipes were evaluated by a panel of food judges and further corrections were made to produce the best flavor, texture and preparation procedures. Please note: although these recipes were developed for high altitude, they will be satisfactory anywhere.

We are confident that these recipes will appeal to both the novice and the experienced cook.

All of them are our favorites!

Evelyn Erdman
Blue Flame Kitchen Director

Contents

Hors D'Oeuvres	1-7
Soups and Salads	8-18
Entrees	19-28
Vegetables	29-35
Breads	36-43
Desserts	44-53
Cakes	54-63
Cookies, Squares & Candies	64-75

For your Information

HIGH ALTITUDE COOKERY
Baked Goods

Lower atmospheric pressure at high altitudes allows leavening in baked goods to expand more. The carbon dioxide gas bubbles released by the leavening become larger and more numerous. The dough or batter walls between the bubbles become thinner and weaker. Without correcting ingredient proportions, the walls of the bubbles may become too thin, collapse and cause the bread or cake to fall.

Moisture vaporizes at a lower temperature, frequently causing an overly dry crumbly texture in baked goods without adjustments.

The internal temperature of a baking cake is much lower at high altitudes. This causes a cake to be underdone when baked for the time specified in an unadjusted recipe.

Adapting Recipes to High Altitude Conditions

1. Yeast Breads: Rise more rapidly at high altitudes and may become overproofed if not watched carefully and allowed to rise only until doubled in bulk. Because flour dries out faster at high altitudes, it may be necessary to use less to make the dough the proper consistency. This will avoid heavy texture.

2. Biscuits, Muffins, Quick Breads: Because of the structure of the product, they will withstand increased internal pressure quite well, so it isn't necessary to vary the ingredients.

3. Cake Batters: For best results:
a) Reduce baking powder or soda by 0.5 mL (⅛ tsp.) for each 5 mL (1 tsp.) called for in the recipe. However, do not reduce the soda beyond 2 mL (½ tsp.) for each 250 mL (1 cup) of sour milk or sour cream used.

b) Reduce the sugar by at least 15 mL (1 tbsp.) for each 250 mL (1 cup) called for in the recipe; the sugar quantity should not greatly exceed half the flour quantity (in a butter-type cake).

c) Add 15-30 mL (1-2 tbsps.) liquid for each 250 mL (1 cup) called for in the recipe.

d) When making a very rich butter or shortening cake, reduce shortening by 15 or 30 mL (1 or 2 tbsps.)

4. Note: In all baked products, with the exception of cookies, time required for baking will be increased. It is advisable not to alter baking temperature. Increase baking times by the following amounts:

Cakes — layer — 8-10 minutes
              square 2-2.5 L (8″ x 8″ or 9″ x 9″) — 15-20 minutes

Quick Breads — approximately 20 minutes

Yeast Breads — at least 15-20 minutes for loaves

5. Pie Crust: is not affected by altitude except for the drying of the flour, so slightly more liquid may be required.

6. Cookies: Usually don't need adjustment, although a slight reduction in baking powder may improve cookies rich in chocoate, nuts or dates. Soda should not be reduced beyond 2 mL (½ tsp.) for each 250 mL (1 cup) sour milk or sour cream used. If drop cookies spread and are too thin and crisp, add 30-50 mL (2 to 4 tbsps.) flour.

7. Boiling Vegetables, Meats, Eggs: Liquids boil at lower temperatures at high altitudes. Because of this, it takes longer to cook vegetables, meats and eggs by boiling.

8. Pressure Cooking: The steam within a pressure cooker is affected by altitude. To reach the temperature desired, the pressure must be increased about 1 lb. for each 2,000 feet elevation. Some cookers will only register 15 lbs. pressure. In this case, cooking time must be increased for each given food.

9. Candies & Frostings: When thermometers are used in making these, remember that sugar solutions, like water, boil at lower temperatures. To determine exact boiling temperatures at a given altitude, check your thermometer in boiling water. The boiling point of the candy can then be determined by first finding the difference between the high altitude reading and sea-level reading for boiling water. The specific candy temperature is then reduced the same number of degrees from the sea-level temperature (that given in a cook book recipe). If this test is carried out prior to every candy-making session, day-to-day variations which occur due to weather conditions will be taken care of.

COMMON FOOD SUBSTITUTIONS

When substituting, remember that some substitutions work well but some work only under special conditions. Never expect to get exactly the same results.

ALLSPICE
5 mL (1 tsp.) = 2 mL (½ tsp.) cinnamon and 2 mL (½ tsp.) ground cloves

BAKING POWDER
5 mL (1 tsp.) = 1.5 mL (⅓ tsp.) baking soda + 2 mL (½ tsp.) cream of tartar

= 1 mL (¼ tsp.) baking soda and 7 mL (½ tbsp.) vinegar or lemon juice used with sweet milk to make 125 mL (½ cup) (decrease liquid called for in recipe by 125 mL (½ cup).)

BUTTERMILK
250 mL (1 cup) = 250 mL (1 cup) yogurt or sour milk

CHOCOLATE
Unsweetened 28 g (1 oz.) = 45 mL (3 tbsps.) cocoa + 7 mL (1½ tsps.) fat

CORNSTARCH
15 mL (1 tbsp.) = 30 mL (2 tbsps.) flour or 15 mL (1 tbsp.) arrowroot or 15 mL (1 tbsp.) potato starch or 30 mL (2 tbsps.) minute tapioca.

CREAM
Sour (Dairy) 250 mL (1 cup) = 65 mL (⅓ cup) butter + 175 mL (¾ cup) sour milk

Heavy (Whipping) 250 mL (1 cup) = 175 mL (¾ cup) milk + 65 mL (⅓ cup) butter (in baking)

Whipped 500 ml (2 cups) = Chill 385 mL (13 fl. oz.) can evaporated milk for 12 hours. Add 5 mL (1 tsp.) lemon juice. Whip until stiff.

FLOUR

250 mL (1 cup) Cake = 250 mL (1 cup) minus 30 mL (2 tbsps.) all-purpose flour

250 mL (1 cup) Self-Raising = 250 mL (1 cup) all-purpose + 7 mL (1½ tsps.) baking powder + 1 mL (¼ tsp.) salt.

GARLIC

0.5 mL (⅛ tsp.) powder = 1 small clove

HERBS

15 mL (1 tbsp.) fresh = 5 mL (1 tsp.) dried

HONEY

See Sugar

MILK

250 mL (1 cup) Sour = 250 mL (1 cup) minus 15 mL (1 tbsp.) lukewarm milk + 15 mL (1 tbsp.) lemon juice or vinegar. Let stand 5 minutes.

SUGAR

250 mL (1 cup) granulated sugar = 250 mL (1 cup) corn syrup minus 50 mL (¼ cup) liquid as replacement of ½ the sugar in recipe.

250 mL (1 cup) granulated sugar = 315 mL (1⅓ cups) molasses minus 75 mL (⅓ cup) liquid + 2 mL (½ tsp.) soda

250 mL (1 cup) granulated sugar = 375 mL (1½ cups) maple syrup minus 50 mL (¼ cup) liquid

250 mL (1 cup) granulated sugar = 175 mL (¾ cup) honey + 1 mL (¼ tsp.) soda less 45 mL (3 tbsps.) liquid

250 mL (1 cup) brown sugar = 250 mL (1 cup) white minus 30 mL (2 tbsps.) + 50 mL (¼ cup) molasses. Let stand 1 hour before using.

COMMON FOOD EQUIVALENTS

BUTTER

500 mL (2 cups) = 454 g (1 lb.)
125 mL (½ cup) = 1 stick

CHOCOLATE

75 mL (⅓ cup) chocolate chips = 56 g (2 oz.) semi-sweet

1 square 28 g (1 oz.) = 60 mL (4 tbsps.) grated

COCOA

1 L (4 cups) = 454 g (1 lb.)

COCONUT

250 mL (1 cup) Fine grated = 3½ oz.

325 mL (1⅓ cups) Flaked = 3½ oz.

1.5 - 1.75 L (6-7 cups) Shredded = 454 g (1 lb.)

CREAM

(whipping) 250 mL (1 cup) = 500 mL (2 cups) whipped

250 mL (1 cup) light cream = 250 mL (1 cup) half and half

DATES

750 mL (3 cups) = 454 g (1 lb.)

EGGS

Whole 4 large, 5 medium, 6 small = 1 cup

Whites, 8-10 = 1 cup

Yolks, 12-14 = 1 cup

FLOUR

All-purpose 1 L (4 cups) = 454 g (1 lb.)

Cake: 1.175 L (4¾ cups) = 454 g (1 lb.)

Rye: 1.125-1.25 L (4½ to 5 cups) = 454 g (1 lb.)

Whole Wheat: 925 mL (3¾ cups) = 454 g (1 lb.)

BLUE FLAME KITCHEN
Homemakers Service

GELATIN
15 mL (1 tbsp.) = 7 g (¼ oz.) pkg. (envelope)

LEMON, MEDIUM SIZE
Juice of 1 = 45 mL (3 tbsps.)

Rind of 1 = 10 to 15 mL (2 to 3 tsps.)

LIME
Juice of 1 = 30 mL (2 tbsps.)

Rind of 1 = 10 mL (2 tsps.)

MACARONI
Elbow – 1 L (4 cups) = 454 g (1 lb.)

MEAT
454 mL (2 cups), diced cooked = 454 g (1 lb.)

MUSHROOMS
Fresh 1.25 L (5 cups) = 454 g (1 lb.)

225 g (½ lb.) = 250 mL (1 cup) cooked, sliced

225 g (½ lb.) = 1 (284 g/10 oz.) can, drained

112 g (¼ lb.) = 175 mL (1¼ cups) chopped or sliced

NUTS
Almonds (whole) 750 mL (3 cups) = 454 g (1 lb.)

Brazil 454 mL (2 cups) = 454 g (1 lb.)

Peanuts 550 mL (2¼ cups) = 454 g (1 lb.)

Walnuts, Pecans 1 L (4 cups) = 454 g (1 lb.)

OATMEAL
2⅔ cups = 454 g (1 lb.)

OATS (rolled)
4¾ cups = 454 g (1 lb.)

ORANGE
Juice of 1 = 125 mL (½ cup)

Rind of 1 = 30-45 mL (2-3 tbsps.)

RAISINS
Seeded 454 mL (2 cups) = 454 g (1 lb.)

Seedless 650 mL (2⅔ cups) = 454 g (1 lb.)

Sultana 675 mL (2¾ cups) = 454 g (1 lb.)

RICE
Uncooked 315 mL (2⅓ cups) = 454 g (1 lb.)

Raw 250 mL (1 cup) = 750 mL (3 cups) cooked

SUGAR
Brown, firmly packed 675 mL (2¾ cups) = 454 g (1 lb.)

Icing 875 mL (3½ cups) = 454 g (1 lb.)

Granulated 454 mL (2 cups) = 454 g (1 lb.)

Berry or Fruit 550 mL (2¼ cups) = 454 g (1 lb.)

TAPIOCA
30 mL (2 tbsps.) granular = 50 mL (4 tbsps.) pearl

YEAST, GRANULAR
15 mL (1 tbsp.) = 7 g (¼ oz.) (1 pkg.)

1 envelope active-dry = 28 g (1 oz.) fresh (1″ x 1″ x 1¼ cube)

1 envelope active-dry = 15 mL (1 tbsp.) active dry

1 envelope active-dry = 10 mL (2 tsps.) rapid mix or quick rise

---

NOTE:
Because flour can become very dry in high altitudes, less flour may be needed in baking, particularly in breads, cookies and squares. Add less flour when making these recipes and add back gradually if needed.

Large eggs were used in all our recipes.

Favorite
Hors D'Oeuvres

LAMB SOSATIES WITH FRUIT

50 mL	oil	¼ cup
375 mL	cider vinegar	1½ cups
45 mL	apricot or pineapple jam	3 tbsps.
25 mL	curry powder	1½ tbsps.
7 mL	salt	1½ tsps.
30 mL	brown sugar, firmly packed	2 tbsps.
1 mL	pepper	¼ tsp.
4	small dried hot chili peppers, crushed (use only 1 or 2 for milder marinade)	4
2	medium-sized onions, sliced	2
3	cloves garlic, mashed	3
2	dried bay leaves	2
2 kg	lean boneless lamb, cubed	4 lbs.
1.5 L	fruit; pitted apricots, pineapple chunks, cantaloupe wedges, and spiced crabapples	6 cups

In a pan combine the oil, vinegar, jam, curry powder, salt, brown sugar, pepper, chili peppers, onions, garlic and bay leaves. Bring to a boil to blend the flavours and cool. Pour the marinade over the meat. Cover and refrigerate 8 to 10 hours or overnight.

Just before you are ready to barbeque the meat, remove the pieces from the marinade and string on skewers. Place the meat over medium-hot coals (medium-high on gas barbecue); grill, turning to brown all sides, a total of 15 to 20 minutes.

Strain the marinade, discarding the onions and leaves; bring liquid to a boil and simmer about 5 minutes to concentrate. Baste the meat occasionally with marinade. String the fruit on skewers. Place on grill for 5 minutes until thoroughly heated, but not soft. Baste with marinade. Serves 8.

2

CHINESE MEATBALLS WITH PLUM SAUCE

500 g	lean ground beef	1 lb.
227 mL	canned water chestnuts	8 oz.
227 mL	canned bamboo shoots	8 oz.
284 mL	canned sliced mushrooms	10 oz.
30 mL	oyster sauce	2 tbsps.
30 mL	soy sauce	2 tbsps.
1	clove garlic, crushed	1
5 mL	ground ginger	1 tsp.
75 mL	sliced green onion	⅓ cup

Preheat oven to 190° C(375° F)

Combine all the ingredients and form small 2.5 cm (1″) balls. Place the meatballs on a wire rack on top of a cookie sheet.

Bake 1 hour or until meatballs have browned.

Serve hot with purchased plum sauce.

Makes 36-40 appetizers.

TACO TARTLETS

500 g	lean ground beef	1 lb.
30 mL	taco seasoning mix	2 tbsps.
30 mL	ice water	2 tbsps.
250 mL	shredded cheddar cheese	1 cup

Tortilla Chip Filling:

250 mL	dairy sour cream	1 cup
30 mL	taco sauce	2 tbsps.
30 mL	chopped ripe olives	2 tbsps.
175 mL	crushed tortilla chips	¾ cup
Preheat oven to 220° C (425° F)		

Combine ingredients for Tortilla Chip Filling; set aside. In a medium bowl, mix beef, taco seasoning mix and ice water with hands. Press into bottom and sides of 2 cm (1″) miniature muffin cups, forming a shell.

Place a spoonful of filling into each shell, mounding slightly. Sprinkle cheddar cheese over tops.

Bake 7 to 8 minutes.

With the tip of a knife remove tartlets from pans. Serve immediately or cool and freeze.

To serve: reheat 10-15 minutes in 190° C (375° F) oven.

Makes 30.

SALMON PÂTÉ

125 g	cream cheese (room temperature)	4 oz.
10 mL	grated onion	2 tsps.
5 mL	lemon juice	1 tsp.
	Dash salt	
2 mL	liquid smoke	½ tsp.
213 g	can salmon, drained, bones and skin removed	7½ oz.
2-5 mL	horseradish	½ - 1 tsp.
	Red food colouring (optional)	

Combine all ingredients, except horseradish, in food processor fitted with metal blade. Process until well blended.

Add horseradish to taste. Spoon into crock; chill several hours before serving. Serve with crackers or cocktail rye bread.

Makes 375 mL (1½ cups).

CHEESY SHRIMP BALLS

250 mL	water	1 cup
125 mL	butter, cut into pieces	½ cup
	Dash salt	
250 mL	flour	1 cup
4	large eggs at room temperature	4
750 mL	grated Gouda cheese	3 cups
125 mL	chopped green onion	½ cup
112 g	can broken shrimp	4 oz.
2 mL	Tabasco sauce	½ tsp.
2 mL	freshly ground pepper	½ tsp.

Place water, butter and salt in a heavy saucepan. Bring to a boil. When butter is completely melted, remove pan from heat and add flour at once.

Mix rapidly with wooden spoon until dough forms a ball and moves freely from the sides of the pan. Do not overmix dough.

Add eggs one at a time beating well after each addition. (Mixture should be smooth before the next egg is added).

Combine remaining ingredients. Add to dough and mix. Drop by teaspoonfuls onto greased cookie sheets and refrigerate or freeze, if desired. (The frozen balls can be packed into freezer bags for future use).

To bake the chilled balls, place in a preheated 200°C (400°F) oven for 20 minutes, reduce temperature to 190°C (375°F) for another 20 minutes or until balls are golden and puffed.

Makes 60 balls.

Note: To bake frozen balls, place on a greased cookie sheet and bake for 30 minutes in a preheated 200°C (400°F) oven. Reduce heat to 190°C (375°F). Bake for an additional 30 minutes or until balls are puffed and browned.

5

6

COUNTRY EGG ROLL TRIANGLES

1	clove garlic, crushed	1
30 ml	oil	2 tbsps.
2	green onions, finely chopped	2
2	carrots, shredded	2
500 ml	fresh bean sprouts	2 cups
198 g	canned broken shrimp, drained	7 oz.
125 mL	finely chopped cooked ham	½ cup
125 mL	butter, melted	½ cup
8 or 10	phyllo pastry sheets approx. 225 g (½ lb.)	8 or 10

Brown garlic in oil. Add onions, carrots and bean sprouts. Stir for 2 to 3 minutes or until sprouts begin to wilt slightly. Remove from heat. Stir in drained shrimp and ham. Mix well. Cool.

Cut phyllo sheets lengthwise into 7 cm (2½ inch) strips. Work with one phyllo strip at a time: keep remaining sheets covered with a damp towel to prevent them from drying out. Brush strip with butter. In one corner of the strip place a heaping 15 mL (1 tbsp.) of the filling. Fold corner over, enclosing filling and forming a triangle at the bottom of the strip. Continue to fold strip maintaining triangular shape. Repeat with remaining strips.

Place "egg roll" triangles on a baking sheet and bake in a preheated 180°C (350°F) oven for 15 minutes or until golden brown.

Serve at once with plum sauce if desired. Makes 20.

*Note: "egg rolls" can be frozen unbaked. Store in airtight plastic. Do not thaw before baking.

SPINACH DIP

300 g	pkg. frozen spinach or broccoli (chopped)	10 oz.
500 mL	sour cream	2 cups
1	pkg. dry leek soup mix	1
250 mL	mayonnaise	1 cup
125 mL	green onions, chopped	½ cup
125 mL	fresh parsley, chopped	½ cup

Thaw spinach or broccoli; drain well.

Put everything in blender or food processor and mix until smooth. Refrigerate overnight.

Hollow out a round loaf of pumpernickel or sourdough bread. Fill with dip.

Serve with bread, crackers, vegetables etc.

Makes 750 mL - 1 L (3-4 cups).

Favorite
Soups & Salads

VEGETABLE SOUP

Metric	Ingredient	Imperial
375 mL	diced carrots, (4 small)	1 ½ cups
175 mL	frozen green peas	¾ cup
250 mL	cauliflower flowerets	1 cup
1	medium potato, diced	1
125 mL	frozen green beans	½ cup
4	small red radishes, halved	4
500 mL	chopped fresh spinach	2 cups
10 mL	salt	2 tsps.
30 mL	butter	2 tbsps.
30 mL	flour	2 tbsps.
250 mL	milk	1 cup
1	egg yolk	1
50 mL	whipping cream	¼ cup
225 g	cooked shrimps or scallops	½ lb.
1 mL	white pepper	¼ tsp.
30 mL	finely chopped fresh parsley or dill	2 tbsps.

Wash, peel and cut vegetables to sizes specified in the ingredient list. Add all vegetables except spinach to a pot and cover with boiling water; add salt. Boil, covered, for about 5 minutes or until vegetables are tender-crisp.

Add spinach and cook another 3 minutes. Remove pan from heat and strain liquid into a bowl and set aside. In a separate pan, melt butter until bubbly, add flour and stir. Remove pan from heat.

Slowly pour in hot vegetable stock beating vigorously with a wire whisk; then beat in milk. In a small bowl, combine egg yolk and cream. Whisk in about a cup of hot soup a little at a time. Now reverse the process and whisk warmed egg yolk and cream mixture back into soup.

Add reserved vegetables to the soup and bring to a simmer. As soon as it comes almost to a boil reduce heat, add cooked shrimp and simmer over low heat 3 to 5 minutes, or until shrimp and vegetables are heated through. Taste and season soup with white pepper and salt. Sprinkle with finely chopped parsley or dill.

Serves 6.

CALCUTTA MULLIGATAWNY SOUP

2 - 2.5 kg	turkey pieces	4 - 5 lb.
75 mL	flour	1/3 cup
75 mL	butter or margarine	1/3 cup
375 mL	chopped onion	1 1/2 cups
500 mL	chopped carrot	2 cups
500 mL	chopped celery	2 cups
375 mL	chopped, pared tart apple	1 1/2 cups
15 mL	curry powder	1 tbsp.
20 mL	salt	4 tsps.
2 mL	nutmeg	1/2 tsp.
2 mL	pepper	1/2 tsp.
1 mL	chili powder	1/4 tsp.
175 mL	flaked coconut	3/4 cup
250 mL	apple juice	1 cup
250 mL	light cream	1 cup
375 mL	hot cooked white rice	1 1/2 cups
125 mL	chopped parsley	1/2 cup

Wash turkey; pat dry with paper towels. Roll turkey in flour, coating completely. Reserve any remaining flour. In hot butter in large kettle or Dutch oven, sauté turkey until well browned on all sides.

Remove from kettle and set aside.

In the same kettle cook onion, carrot, celery, apple and any remaining flour 5 minutes, stirring constantly.

Add curry powder, salt, nutmeg, pepper, chili powder, coconut, turkey and 1.5 L (6 cups) water. Mix well. Bring to boiling; reduce heat and simmer, covered, two hours. Stir occasionally. Remove from heat. Skim fat from soup. Remove skin and bone from turkey. Cut turkey meat into large pieces; set aside. Put soup through blender. Return to kettle, with turkey. Stir in apple juice and light cream; reheat. To serve: place 25 mL (1 heaping tablespoon) rice in each of 6 to 8 bowls. Add soup. Sprinkle each serving with parsley.

Serves 6-8.

BAKED MINESTRONE

1 kg	lean stewing beef	2 lbs.
250 mL	coarsely chopped onion	1 cup
2	cloves garlic crushed	2
5 mL	salt	1 tsp.
2 mL	black pepper	½ tsp.
30 mL	olive oil	2 tbsps.
1.5 L	beef stock (homemade or canned)	1 ½ qts.
2 mL	basil	½ tsp.
398 mL	can kidney beans, undrained	14 oz.
398 mL	can tomatoes	14 oz.
250 mL	thinly sliced carrots	1 cup
250 mL	small uncooked macaroni	1 cup
500 mL	sliced zucchini	2 cups
	Grated Parmesan cheese	

Mix beef, onion, garlic, salt and pepper in a large saucepan.

Add olive oil and brown over medium heat.

Preheat oven to 180°C (350°F).

Add stock and basil; stir. Cover; place in oven, cook 2 hours or until meat is tender.

Stir in kidney beans, tomatoes, carrots, and macaroni. Put sliced zucchini on top. Cover; bake 60 minutes longer, or until carrots are tender.

Serve with grated cheese.

Serves 10 - 12.

SEAFOOD SOUP

2	medium onions, chopped	2
3	garlic cloves, crushed	3
50 mL	olive oil	¼ cup
3	medium tomatoes, chopped	3
225 g	clam nectar	8 oz.
500 mL	chicken broth	2 cups
1 L	water	4 cups
10 mL	salt	2 tsps.
2 mL	thyme	½ tsp.
2 mL	crushed fennel seed	½ tsp.
2 mL	turmeric	½ tsp.
1	bay leaf	1
2 kg	white fish (cod, haddock, flounder, or sole) cut into 2.5 cm (1") cubes	4 lbs.
	OR a combination of:	
500 g	white fish	1 lb.
250 g	shrimp	½ lb.
2 - 142 g	cans clams with juice	2 - 5 oz.

Cook and stir together onions and garlic in oil until onions are tender. Add remaining ingredients except seafood.

Heat to boiling; reduce heat. Cover and cook 5 minutes. Add seafood to soup mixture. Heat to boiling; reduce heat.

Cover and cook until fish flakes easily with fork, about 5 minutes. Serve with toasted French bread.

Serves 8.

WHITE BEAN & HAM SOUP

454 g	white beans	1 lb.
15 mL	oil	1 tbsp.
250 mL	chopped onion	1 cup
1-2	cloves garlic, crushed	1-2
500 mL	thinly sliced celery	2 cups
2 L	water	2 qts.
125 mL	dry white wine	½ cup
1	ham bone	1
250 mL	cubed left-over ham	1 cup
30 mL	fresh lemon juice	2 tbsps.
50 mL	anise-flavoured liqueur	¼ cup
5-10 mL	salt	1-2 tsps.
1 mL	freshly ground pepper	¼ tsp.
50 mL	chopped parsley	¼ cup

Cover beans with water; soak overnight in refrigerator. Drain beans well. In a large soup pot, heat oil and sauté onions and garlic until tender. Stir in celery and sauté a few minutes longer. Add water, wine, ham bone, ham and beans. Bring to boil. Reduce heat, and simmer until beans are very tender and meat falls off bone (approximately 3 hours).

Remove bone from soup and carefully remove any remaining meat (do not include gristle). Return meat to soup and season with lemon juice, liqueur, salt and pepper. Just before serving stir in parsley. Serves 8 to 10.

13

SHRIMP & CUCUMBER RING

175 g	lime jelly powder (pkg.)	6 oz.
5 mL	plain gelatin	1 tsp.
500 mL	boiling water	2 cups
50 mL	lemon juice	¼ cup
125 mL	cold water	½ cup
1 small	cucumber, sliced	1
500 mL	sour cream	2 cups
10 mL	grated onion	2 tsps.
375 mL	finely chopped cucumber	1 ½ cups
250 mL	cooked shrimp	1 cup
2 mL	salt	½ tsp.

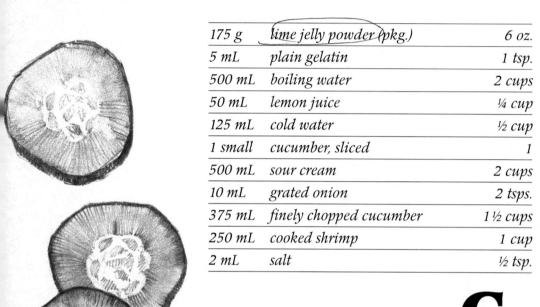

Combine lime jelly powder and plain gelatin in large bowl. Add boiling water and stir until gelatin dissolves. Add lemon juice.

Measure 125 mL (½ cup) of this mixture into a large bowl and set aside. Chill remainder until the thickness of raw egg white. Combine cold water with the 125 mL (½ cup) of gelatin mixture. Brush 1.5 L (6 cup) mold with oil. Cover the bottom of ring mold with ½ of this mixture. Chill until almost set.

Overlap thin cucumber slices on gelatin. Carefully cover with remaining gelatin mixture. Chill until almost set.

Meanwhile into syrupy gelatin in large bowl, fold in sour cream, onion, chopped cucumber, shrimp and salt. Spoon mixture carefully into mold over cucumber layer. Chill until firm. Unmold onto serving plate lined with crisp greens.

Serves 10 to 12.

FRUIT & CABBAGE SLAW

2	oranges, peeled and sectioned	2
2	apples, chopped, unpeeled	2
500 mL	shredded cabbage	2 cups
250 mL	seedless green grapes	1 cup

Dressing:

125 mL	whipping cream, whipped	½ cup
15 mL	sugar	1 tbsp.
15 mL	lemon juice	1 tbsp.
1 mL	salt	¼ tsp.
125 mL	mayonnaise	½ cup

Combine salad ingredients in serving bowl.

In separate bowl fold whipped cream, sugar, lemon juice and salt into mayonnaise. Stir into fruit mixture.

Serves 6.

15

ORANGE CHICKEN SALAD WITH ALMONDS

Dressing:

50 mL	fresh parsley, minced	¼ cup
50 mL	oil	¼ cup
50 mL	frozen orange juice, concentrate	¼ cup
15 mL	red wine vinegar	1 tbsp.
5 mL	prepared mustard	1 tsp.
1	egg	1
5 mL	salt (optional)	1 tsp.
	dash hot pepper sauce	
	fresh ground pepper	

Salad:

2	whole chicken breasts, cooked and skinned	2
3	celery stalks, julienne	3
1	romaine lettuce, shredded	1
1	red pepper, julienne	1
3	green onions, including tops, sliced	3
125 mL	toasted sliced almonds	½ cup
1	large seedless orange, scored and sliced	1
	parsley for garnish	

Combine ingredients for salad dressing. Set aside.

Cut chicken into bite-size slices. Transfer to large bowl. Add celery, lettuce, red pepper, green onions and almonds. Pour on dressing and toss gently. Mound salad on large serving platter and surround with orange slices. Arrange parsley sprigs between salad and orange slices. Serve immediately.

Serves 4-6.

LEMON LETTUCE WEDGES

250 mL	mayonnaise and/or sour cream and/or yogurt	1 cup
2 mL	curry powder	½ tsp.
10 mL	freshly grated lemon peel	2 tsps.
50 mL	fresh lemon juice	¼ cup
1	head of lettuce	1
2	tomatoes, sliced	2
1	green pepper, sliced	1

Combine mayonnaise, curry powder, lemon peel, and lemon juice; refrigerate 4 to 6 hours.

Cut lettuce into 8-10 wedges and serve garnished with sliced tomato and green pepper. Pour 30 mL (2 tbsps.) dressing over each serving. Serves 8-10.

17 FIRE & ICE TOMATOES

6	tomatoes, large, ripe, firm	6
1	green pepper	1
1	red onion	1
1	cucumber	1

Marinade:

175 mL	vinegar	¾ cup
7 mL	mustard seed	1 ½ tsps.
25 mL	sugar	5 tsps.
0.5 mL	black pepper	⅛ tsp.
7 mL	celery salt	1 ½ tsps.
2 mL	salt	½ tsp.
0.5 mL	cayenne pepper	⅛ tsp.
50 mL	water	¼ cup

Combine marinade ingredients in a saucepan. Slowly bring to a boil over low heat, then boil vigorously but only for 1 minute. Set aside, keeping it hot.

Meanwhile, skin and quarter tomatoes. Slice green pepper into strips and slice red onion into rings. Place in a bowl. Pour hot marinade over tomatoes, green pepper and onion. Cool.

Just before serving, add peeled and sliced cucumber. Without the addition of the cucumber, this salad will store in the refrigerator for 2 or 3 days.

Serves 6 to 8.

OLD FASHIONED POTATO SALAD

10	potatoes	10
1 stalk	celery, diced	1 stalk
½	green pepper, diced	½
2	tomatoes, peeled, seeded and chopped	2
125 mL	diced green onions	½ cup
500 mL	boiled salad dressing (recipe follows)	2 cups
225 g	bacon, cooked and diced	½ lb.
	salt and pepper	

Boil potatoes, peel and dice. Add all other ingredients, toss and chill together 2-4 hours before serving. Serves 8-10.

Boiled Salad Dressing

30 mL	flour	2 tbsps.
7 mL	salt	1 ½ tsps.
4 mL	dry mustard	¾ tsp.
30 mL	sugar	2 tbsps.
1 mL	paprika	¼ tsp.
2	egg yolks	2
30 mL	butter, melted	2 tbsps.
300 mL	milk	1 ¼ cups
75 mL	vinegar	⅓ cup

Combine dry ingredients in top of a double boiler. Stir in egg yolks, butter and milk. Cook over boiling water, stirring constantly until mixture begins to thicken, stir in vinegar. When thickened remove from heat and cool.

Makes 500 mL (2 cups).

Favorite Entrees

BACON-STUFFED TROUT

2	eggs	2
15 mL	cream or milk	1 tbsp.
15 mL	chopped fresh parsley	1 tbsp.
1	clove garlic, minced	1
2 mL	allspice	½ tsp.
8	cleaned trout	8
8-16	strips of grilled bacon	8-16
	lemon wedges	
	parsley	

Beat together first 5 ingredients to blend. Coat fish inside and out with mixture. Put one or two strips grilled bacon in each trout and place in greased wire broil basket or on greased hot grid. Barbecue over medium to high flame setting for 15 to 20 minutes, turning fish once. (Fish flakes with a fork when cooked).

Serve with lemon wedges and garnish with parsley.

Serves 8.

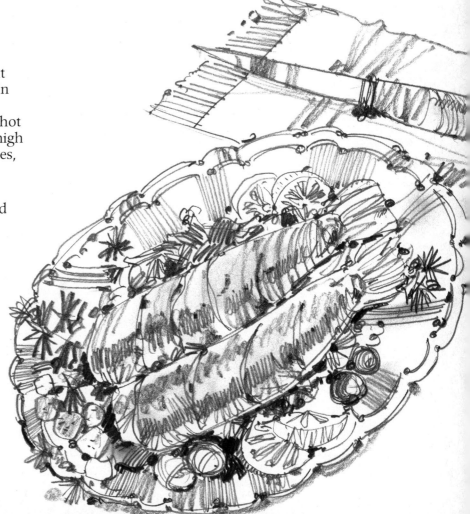

ROAST BEEF & NEVER FAIL YORKSHIRE PUDDING

PREPARATION:

Bring roast to room temperature. A chilled roast taken directly from the refrigerator to the oven will cook unevenly. Trim fat evenly without exposing meat. Cuts of meat that lack a protective fat covering should be coated with oil or a thin layer of fat prior to roasting to prevent drying out.

Season roast with salt and pepper *just before* it goes into a hot oven to prevent juices from being drawn out. Insert a meat thermometer into the thickest part of the roast, making sure it doesn't touch fat or bone.

The roasting pan should be about an inch larger all the way around than the meat. If the pan is too large, the pan drippings can burn; if the pan is too small, the roast can steam in its own juices instead of roasting. Use a rack under the roast to prevent stewing.

ROASTING:

Preheat the oven and empty roasting pan to a hot temperature 260°C (500°F) in order to seal in the juices and brown the meat. Place meat in hot roasting pan into hot oven for 15 minutes. Lower temperature to 180°C (350°F).

Roast to: 60°C (120°F) rare; 75°C (135°F) medium*; (150°F) well done. The time the roast will take to cook is based on minutes per pound.

This is a rough guide since timing will vary with the individual piece of meat. Remove roast when done. Avoid piercing the meat. *Let roast rest for 20 minutes* to redistribute juices.

*Rib Roast with bone in: 20 minutes per pound for 70°C (135°F)

*Top Round Rolled Boneless Roast: 35 minutes per pound for 70°C (135°F)

NEVER FAIL YORKSHIRE PUDDING

Preheat oven to 230° C (450° F)

250 mL	*flour*	*1 cup*
2 mL	*salt*	*½ tsp.*
125 mL	*milk*	*½ cup*
125 mL	*water*	*½ cup*
2	*eggs*	*2*
	Solid fat	

Combine flour and salt into a 500 mL (2 cup) *glass* measuring cup. Make a well in the center and pour in milk, water and eggs. Stir together just until all ingredients are blended. Put 2 mL (½ tsp.) hot beef drippings or melted butter (not oil) in each cup of a 12 cup muffin tin. PREHEAT PAN UNTIL FAT IS BUBBLY BUT NOT SMOKING. FILL PANS WHILE ON OVEN RACK TO PREVENT EXCESSIVE COOLING DOWN.

Pour in about 50 mL (¼ cup) batter into each muffin cup. Bake at 230° C (450° F) for 20 minutes. Reduce heat to 180° C (350° F) and bake 10-15 minutes longer. Do not open oven door while baking. Serve at once. Makes 12.

21

THREE CHEESE MEATLOAF IN PUFF PASTRY

2-215 g	packages frozen puff pastry	2-8 oz.
1 kg	lean ground beef	2 lbs.
500 mL	finely chopped onion	2 cups
1	clove garlic, finely chopped	1
500 mL	thawed spinach finely chopped	2 cups
125 mL	grated Parmesan cheese	½ cup
30 mL	finely chopped fresh parsley	2 tbsps.
2	eggs, lightly beaten	2
3	slices bread soaked in 125 mL (½ cup) milk drained and squeezed	3
10 mL	salt	2 tsps.
	freshly ground pepper	
250 mL	finely cubed mozzarella cheese	1 cup
250 mL	grated Gruyere cheese	1 cup

Combine meat, onions, garlic, spinach, Parmesan cheese, parsley, eggs, bread, salt and pepper in a large bowl and blend well.

Divide mixture into 3 portions. Pat ⅓ of mixture into bottom of a 2 L (9"x5"x3") loaf pan. Sprinkle mozzarella cubes over top. Add another ⅓ meat mixture; cover with grated Gruyere. Add remaining ⅓ meat mixture patting in place to edge of pan.

Roll out puff pastry to a 44 cm (17") square. Carefully remove the meatloaf onto centre of the rolled out pastry. Wrap pastry around the meatloaf and seal ends and middle seam using a small amount of water to moisten the edges. Carefully place pastry-wrapped meatloaf seam side down onto an ungreased jellyroll pan. Cut a few small vent holes in top of pastry to make an eye-appealing pattern. Brush pastry with a lightly beaten egg. Bake in 190°C (375°F) oven for 1 hour to 1¼ hours or until pastry is golden brown.

Serves 12.

SEAFOOD LASAGNE

454 g	sole fillets	1 lb.
198 g	scallops	7 oz.
142 g	canned crabmeat, drained	5 oz.
20	lasagne noodles	20
300 mL	grated Parmesan cheese	1¼ cups
250 mL	Italian-style tomato sauce, optional	1 cup

Sauce:

125 mL	finely chopped onion	½ cup
3	cloves garlic, crushed	3
125 mL	sliced celery	½ cup
75 mL	butter	⅓ cup
750 mL	sliced mushrooms	3 cups
75 mL + 15 mL	flour	⅓ c. + 1 tbsp.
125 mL	dry white wine	½ cup
1 L	half and half cream	4 cups
125 mL	chopped parsley	½ cup

Sauce: In a 3L (3 qt.) saucepan saute onions, garlic and celery in butter until tender. Add mushrooms and saute until moisture is released from mushrooms and they are slightly brown. Add flour to vegetables and stir to combine. Cook until bubbly. While stirring, pour in wine and cream and cook until thickened, stirring constantly. Stir in parsley.

Thaw sole and scallops, if necessary. Cut into bite-sized pieces and combine with drained crabmeat. Cook lasagne noodles just until pliable (3 to 4 minutes).

Preheat oven to 180°C (350°F).

To assemble lasagne: Lightly butter a 3.5 L (13" x 9") utility pan. Pour in approximately 250 mL (1 cup) of sauce and spread evenly over the bottom. Layer with 4 lasagne noodles. Spread with ¼ of the seafood mixture, 50 mL (¼ cup) Parmesan cheese and 500 mL (2 cups) sauce. Repeat layering until all seafood is used, finishing with a layer of noodles. Cover with remaining sauce and cheese. If desired, sprinkle with parsley. Cover with aluminum foil and bake for 1 hour. Allow lasagne to rest, uncovered for 15 minutes before cutting. If desired, heat Italian-style tomato sauce, and serve the lasagne garnished with 15 to 30 mL (1 to 2 tbsps.) of the heated sauce for each serving.

Serves 8 to 12.

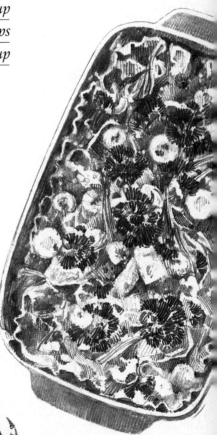

23

MAPLE FLAVORED RIBS

Pork spareribs: Estimate 500 g (1 lb.) per person served.

Sauce & Marinade

125 mL	maple syrup	½ cup
50 mL	soy sauce	¼ cup
125 mL	chili sauce	½ cup
2	cloves garlic, mashed	2
125 mL	sherry	½ cup

Combine all ingredients for marinade and stir to mix well. Makes 500 mL (2 cups) sufficient to marinate 1 kg. (2 lbs.) spareribs. Simmer ribs for 20-30 minutes in large pot of water. Drain and dry with paper towelling. Place the ribs in a large dish and pour the marinade over. Marinate for 2 hours at room temperature or overnight in the refrigerator. Turn the ribs frequently.

To Barbecue Ribs: Cook on grids of preheated barbecue over low to medium heat, turning frequently for 30-45 minutes or until well-done. Baste with remaining marinade during last 15 minutes to enhance flavor.

A whole strip of ribs can also be cooked on the rotisserie by weaving the strip accordion-style on the spit. Take care that the ribs are balanced on the rod and that they are not packed too tightly. Cook over low to medium heat in a preheated gas barbecue for 30-45 minutes or until sufficiently cooked.

To Bake Ribs: Preheat oven to 200°C (400°F) or use broiler. Place ribs in a shallow pan suitable for baking. Baste frequently with sauce and broil or bake until browned 15-30 minutes or until sufficiently cooked.

STUFFED PORK WITH CURRY SAUCE

250 g	dried apricots	8 oz.
500 g	bulk sausage	1 lb.
1	medium onion, finely chopped	1
30 mL	chopped parsley	2 tbsps.
2 mL	thyme	½ tsp.
2 mL	marjoram	½ tsp.
	salt	
	pepper	
15 mL	vegetable oil	1 tbsp.
250 mL	dry bread crumbs	1 cup
2 kg	boneless pork loin roast	4 lbs.
5 mL	paprika	1 tsp.

Sauce:

75 mL	mayonnaise	⅓ cup
10-15 mL	curry powder	2-3 tsps.
75 mL	whipping cream	⅓ cup
	a pinch of sugar	

Soak 15 apricots 2-3 hours in warm water. Reserve for sauce. Chop remaining apricots. Set aside.

Combine sausage, onion, parsley, thyme, marjoram, salt and pepper. Heat oil in medium skillet. Add sausage mixture. Cook, stirring constantly, until well browned. Remove from heat; add chopped apricots and bread crumbs.

Remove string from roast, unroll. Cut away any excess fat. Stuff pork with sausage mixture; reroll and tie. Sprinkle surface with paprika. If desired, cover roast with trimmed fat. Roast 2 hours at 160°C (325°F) or until meat thermometer inserted in pork registers 80°C (170°F).

To make sauce: Drain reserved apricots. Puree. In a small bowl combine puree with remaining ingredients. Serve with roast. Serves 8.

JAMBALAYA

225 g	stewing beef (cut into 2.5 cm/1" cubes)	8 oz.
	salt and freshly ground pepper	
125 mL	bacon drippings	½ cup
1-1.5 kg	rack, pork spareribs (cut into 2.5 cm/1" strips)	2½-3 lbs.
2	medium onions, chopped	2
6	green onions, chopped	6
50 mL	minced fresh parsley	¼ cup
3	cloves garlic, minced	3
500 mL	uncooked long-grain rice	2 cups
1 L	chicken stock	4 cups
454 g	Bavarian sausage, cut into chunks	1 lb.
10 mL	salt	2 tsps.
4 mL	cayenne	¾ tsp.

Season beef with salt and pepper. Melt bacon drippings in heavy, very large saucepan over medium-high heat until very hot.

Pat beef dry. Separate ribs and pat dry. Add beef and ribs to pan in batches and brown well. Remove and set aside. Add onions, parsley and garlic to pan and stir until tender. Blend in rice and stir until golden. Pour in stock. Add beef, ribs, sausage, salt and cayenne. Bring to boil, stirring constantly. Reduce heat to low, cover tightly and cook 45 minutes. Check rice for tenderness; if mixture appears dry, but rice is not yet tender, add more stock and continue cooking. Turn mixture into bowl and fluff with fork. Serve immediately.

Serves 8.

HONEY ORANGE SPICED CHICKEN

30 mL	vegetable oil	2 tbsps.
1-1.5 kg	chicken, cut up	2½-3 lbs.
2	medium onions	2
5 mL	salt	1 tsp.
5 mL	paprika	1 tsp.
1 mL	pepper	¼ tsp.
125 mL	pitted ripe olives	½ cup
250 mL	orange juice	1 cup
50 mL	honey	¼ cup
30 mL	lemon juice	2 tbsps.
2 mL	ground ginger	½ tsp.
1 mL	ground nutmeg	¼ tsp.
30 mL	cold water	2 tbsps.
10 mL	cornstarch	2 tsps.
	orange slices	

Heat oil in skillet until hot. Cook chicken over medium heat until brown on all sides, about 15 minutes. Place chicken in one layer in an ungreased baking dish. Slice onions thinly. Sprinkle chicken with salt, paprika, pepper and top with sliced onions and olives. Mix orange juice, honey, lemon juice, ginger, nutmeg; pour over chicken.

Cover and cook in 180° C (350° F) oven until thickest pieces of chicken are done, 45 to 60 minutes.

Arrange chicken, onions and olives on platter. Pour pan juices into saucepan; heat to boiling. Mix water and cornstarch; stir into juices. Cook and stir until slightly thickened, 1-2 minutes. Garnish chicken with orange slices; serve with orange sauce. 6 to 8 servings.

27

SPINACH-STUFFED CHICKEN LEGS

6	chicken legs with thighs, deboned	6

Stuffing:

300 g pkg.	frozen chopped spinach, thawed	10 oz.
30 mL	butter	2 tbsps.
250 mL	finely chopped onion	1 cup
5 mL	liquid beef bouillon concentrate	1 tsp.
15 mL	soy sauce	1 tbsp.
250 mL	sour cream	1 cup
250 mL	seasoned croutons	1 cup

27

Coating:

250 mL	flour	1 cup
2 mL	salt	½ tsp.
2 mL	freshly ground pepper	½ tsp.
1 mL	freshly ground nutmeg	¼ tsp.
2	eggs	2
15 mL	water	1 tbsp.
550 mL	fine dry bread crumbs	2 ¼ cups
	Oil for frying	

To debone chicken: Place pieces skin-side down on a work surface. Using the point of a sharp knife, cut along full length of bone. Repeat on other side of bone keeping meat in one piece. Insert knife under end of bone in thigh portion. Cut completely under the bone removing it from the meat. Remove any tendons or cartilage. Repeat for leg section keeping meat in one piece. Smooth leg and thigh piece into original shape.

To make stuffing: Squeeze spinach to remove all moisture. In a medium-sized skillet, melt butter and brown onions. Add bouillon and soy sauce. Remove from heat and allow to cool. Stir in sour cream and croutons.

To assemble: Distribute filling evenly among the 6 deboned chicken leg-thighs. Overlap skin and press firmly together to enclose stuffing. Secure with a wooden skewer if desired. In a pie plate, combine flour, salt, pepper and nutmeg. In a shallow bowl, beat eggs with water. Spread bread crumbs in a second pie plate.

Roll chicken pieces in seasoned flour. Shake off excess. Dip floured chicken pieces in egg mixture; drain over bowl then roll chicken pieces in bread crumbs. Press bread crumbs evenly onto chicken. Place coated chicken on a wire rack. Refrigerate for 30 minutes to firm coating. Place 2 cm (¾") of oil in a pan suitable for frying. Heat oil to 175°C (350°F). Brown chicken pieces two at a time, turning with tongs. Drain on paper towels. Place chicken pieces on rack suitable for baking. Bake in preheated 175°C (350°F) oven for 20 minutes or until done. When done meat should be white but still moist.

Makes 6 servings.

BARBECUED STUFFED LEG OF LAMB

2.5-3 kg	leg of lamb, boned and butterflied	5-6 lbs.

Seasonings:

10 mL	salt	2 tsps.
5 mL	dried thyme, crushed	1 tsp.
5 mL	ground coriander	1 tsp.
2 mL	pepper	½ tsp.

Marinade:

75 mL	cooking oil	⅓ cup
75 mL	lemon juice	⅓ cup
50 mL	minced onion	¼ cup
2	cloves garlic, minced	2

Stuffing:

425 mL	dried wholewheat bread crumbs or cracked wheat bread crumbs	1 ¾ cup
2	stalks celery, finely diced	2
2	cooking apples, cored and diced	2
150 mL	well-drained, crushed pineapple	⅔ cup
75 mL	seedless raisins	⅓ cup
5-7 mL	curry powder	1 ½-2 tsps.
5 mL	onion powder	1 tsp.
5 mL	salt	1 tsp.
50 mL	butter, melted	¼ cup

Condiments:

250 mL	plain yogurt	1 cup
2	medium tomatoes, chopped	2
250 mL	snipped fresh parsley	1 cup

With meat mallet, pound the lamb to a 40 cm x 30 cm (16″ x 12″) rectangle, 1.25 cm - 2 cm (½″ - ¾″) thick. Pound only on cut surface. Cut and patch meat where necessary to make surface uniform. Combine seasonings; sprinkle over cut surface of lamb. Pound in seasonings. Combine marinade ingredients; pour over lamb in a shallow pan or plastic bag. Cover; chill several hours or overnight, turning occasionally.

Day of Barbecue: Remove meat from marinade (most of the liquid should be absorbed). Combine all stuffing ingredients. Place lamb, cut side up, on work surface. Evenly spread stuffing on cut surface of meat, leaving a 1.25 cm (½″) border around edges (so the stuffing won't fall out). With a rolling pin, press stuffing into a flat layer. Roll meat up, beginning at narrow end. Tie securely with string, first in centre, then halfway to each end. Tie lengthwise. Finish securing the roll by tying once more between crosswise strings. Insert the rotisserie rod through the centre of the meat and test balance. Fasten the meat with holding forks.

Preheat gas barbecue on high for 10 minutes. Adjust flame to medium and attach the spit; turn on motor. Place a drip pan under meat. Roast with hood partially down, for about 2 hours, or until done.

Remove from spit. Allow to rest 15 mintues. Slice meat and serve with yogurt, tomato and parsley.

Serves 6-8.

Favorite Vegetables

COINTREAU CARROT COINS

1 L	carrots, sliced into coins	4 cups
30 mL	Cointreau, or any orange-flavoured liqueur	2 tbsps.
75 mL	fresh lemon juice	⅓ cup
45 mL	brandy	3 tbsps.
50 mL	honey	¼ cup
15 mL	parsley, finely chopped	1 tbsp.

Simmer carrots in boiling salted water until tender crisp; drain.

Arrange in a single layer in a buttered baking dish.

Blend together Cointreau, lemon juice, brandy and honey; pour over carrots and bake in 180°C (350°F) oven for 10 minutes.

Baste several times. Sprinkle with parsley and serve.

Serves 8 to 10.

PEPPER PEA POD SKILLET

30 mL	oil	2 tbsps.
15 mL	soy sauce	1 tbsp.
5 mL	ginger	1 tsp.
5 mL	salt	1 tsp.
2	red peppers, cleaned and trimmed	2
500 mL	pea pods	2 cups
350 g	mushrooms	12 oz.
50 mL	chicken stock	¼ cup
50 mL	water	¼ cup
30 mL	cornstarch	2 tbsps.

Heat oil in skillet. Add soy sauce, ginger and salt. Stir-fry red peppers with pea pods until tender-crisp. Remove from pan. Set aside.

Add sliced mushrooms. Stir-fry one minute. Add chicken stock. Mix water with cornstarch and add to mushroom mixture. Mix until sauce thickens. Add pea pods and peppers. Stir well together until mixed thoroughly.

Serves 6.

RATATOUILLE

2	medium onions, sliced	2
1	green pepper, sliced	1
75 mL	olive oil	⅓ cup
2	cloves garlic, minced	2
1	medium eggplant, peeled and chopped	1
3	large tomatoes, skinned, seeded and chopped	3
30 mL	tomato paste	2 tbsps.
5 mL	basil	1 tsp.
30 mL	parsley, chopped	2 tbsps.
1 mL	pepper	¼ tsp.
2	zucchini, thinly sliced	2
5 mL	salt	1 tsp.
250 mL	mushrooms, sliced or whole	1 cup

Combine onions, green pepper, oil and garlic in 2 L (2 qt.) casserole and heat, FULL POWER in a microwave or 15 minutes in a 190°C (375°F) conventional oven. Add remaining ingredients, heat, covered 18 to 20 minutes in microwave on FULL POWER, stirring occasionally or for 45 to 60 minutes in the hot oven.

Let stand covered, 5 minutes and serve.

Ratatouille is excellent served cold or reheated with 250 mL (1 cup) grated Gruyere or cheddar cheese.

Serves 8 to 10.

LEMON SWEET POTATOES

2-796 mL	cans sweet potatoes	2-26 fl. oz.
	OR	
1.5 kg	cooked and peeled fresh sweet potatoes	3 lbs.
50 mL	fresh lemon juice	¼ cup
5 mL	salt	1 tsp.
50 mL	butter, melted	¼ cup
2	egg yolks	2
	grated rind of 1 lemon	
	pepper to taste	
	lemon slices	
	parsley	
	preheat oven to 160° C (325°F)	

Mash sweet potatoes. Add lemon juice, salt, melted butter, egg yolks, lemon rind and pepper. Transfer mixture to a buttered 1.5 L (1½ quart) casserole dish. Bake casserole covered 45 minutes or until heated through. Garnish with lemon slices and parsley.

Serves 8.

SPANAKOPITTA

33

2 (300 g) pkgs.	frozen chopped spinach	2 (10 oz.) pkgs.
30 mL	butter	2 tbsps.
1	small onion, chopped	1
50 mL	chopped green onion	¼ cup
30 mL	finely chopped fresh parsley	2 tbsps.
5 mL	dill weed	1 tsp.
1 mL	pepper	¼ tsp.
50 mL	milk	¼ cup
3	eggs	3
125 g	feta cheese	¼ lb.
250 g	phyllo pastry	½ lb.
250 mL	melted butter	1 cup

Thaw spinach and squeeze out as much water as possible. Saute onion in 30 mL (2 tbsps.) butter until golden brown. Add green onion and cook until wilted. Add spinach and seasonings. Toss lightly. Remove from heat and add milk. Beat eggs lightly in another bowl and add feta cheese, coarsely crumbled. Add to spinach mixture and mix well. With a pastry brush, coat bottom and sides of a 2.5 L (11x7x2 inch) baking dish with melted butter. Line with 8 sheets of phyllo, brushing each sheet with melted butter. Do not trim overhanging sections. Pour in spinach mixture and fold overhanging sections back over filling. Top with 8 sheets of phyllo, brush each sheet with butter. Trim overlap. Brush top with butter and score into squares or diamonds. Bake in a 180°C (350°F) oven for 45 minutes. Let stand 10 minutes before serving.

Serves 8-12.

34

POTATO PINWHEELS

Filling:

Metric	Ingredient	Imperial
1.5 kg	potatoes, peeled and cut into 1.25 cm (½") cubes (approx. 12)	3 lbs.
30 mL	butter	2 tbsps.
2	medium onions, finely chopped	2
1	clove garlic, crushed	1
1 mL	freshly ground pepper	¼ tsp.
7 mL	salt	1 ½ tsps.

Pastry:

Metric	Ingredient	Imperial
500 mL	flour	2 cups
2 mL	salt	½ tsp.
175 mL	shortening	¾ cup
50 mL	ice water	¼ cup
2	egg yolks, beaten (for glaze)	2

Cook potatoes until tender. While potatoes are cooking, brown onions and garlic in butter. Mash potatoes and add cooked onion-garlic mixture, salt and pepper. Set aside.

Pastry

Combine flour and salt in a large bowl. Cut shortening into flour until it resembles coarse crumbs. Sprinkle ice water over crumb mixture a little at a time, tossing with a fork until dough forms a ball. Divide in half.

On a floured surface roll out half the dough into 30 cm (12") square. Spread half the potato mixture over the pastry leaving a 1.25 cm (½") strip of pastry uncovered on one long side. Roll pastry, jelly roll fashion towards the uncovered edge of pastry. Spread some water on this strip and seal it to the roll. Cut into 2.5 cm (1") slices and place 5 cm (2") apart on lightly greased cookie sheet. Brush with the beaten egg yolk. Repeat process with remaining pastry and potato mixture. Bake in preheated 230°C (450°F) oven for 15 minutes or until golden brown.

Serves 12.

BROCCOLI STUFFED POTATOES

6	large baker potatoes	6
284 g pkg.	frozen broccoli, thawed and finely chopped	10 oz.
50 mL	butter	¼ cup
75 mL	finely chopped onion	⅓ cup
125 mL	finely chopped mushrooms	½ cup
4 mL	salt	¾ tsp.
2 mL	rosemary	½ tsp.
1 mL	pepper	¼ tsp.
125 mL	plain yogurt	½ cup
125 mL	mayonnaise	½ cup

Topping:

30 mL	butter	2 tbsps.
125 mL	bread crumbs	½ cup
50 mL	sliced almonds (optional)	¼ cup

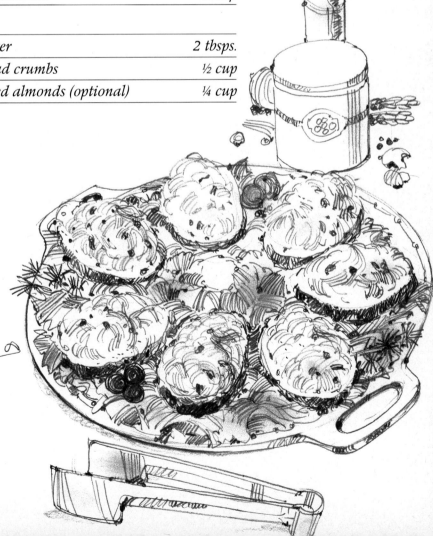

Bake potatoes at 200° C (400° F) until tender, about 1 hour. To prepare broccoli stuffing: thoroughly drain thawed broccoli. Set aside. In large skillet; melt butter over medium heat and saute onions for 1 to 2 minutes. Stir in mushrooms, salt, rosemary, and pepper; cook gently for 3-4 minutes or until vegetables are tender. Mix in broccoli, set aside. Cut slice from top of each potato. Scoop out pulp, reserving shells, and transfer to large bowl. Mash pulp and stir in broccoli mixture, yogurt and mayonnaise. Taste and adjust seasoning. Spoon mixture into potato shells, mounding slightly. Place on oven-proof platter.

Topping: In skillet melt butter; mix in bread crumbs and almonds; saute until crisp and golden, a few minutes. Sprinkle evenly over stuffed potatoes. Bake at 180° C (350° F) until heated through, 20-25 minutes. Serves 6.

Favorite Breads

SWEET DOUGH-QUICK RISE

1.5-1.75 L	flour	6-7 cups
30mL	*quick rising yeast	2 tbsps.
750 mL	water	3 cups
125 mL	sugar	½ cup
75 mL	oil	⅓ cup
2	eggs, beaten	2
5 mL	salt	1 tsp.

*Brand names: Fermipan, Fleishman's Quick Rise

In a large bread bowl, combine the yeast with 1 L (4 cups) of flour. In a saucepan combine the water, sugar, oil and eggs and beat well.

Heat the liquid mixture, stirring constantly, to 85°-90°C (120°-130°F). Add the heated liquid to the flour-yeast mixture and stir the batter well for 4-5 minutes.

Combine 250 mL (1 cup) flour with the salt and stir it into the batter. Add only enough remaining flour to make a soft dough.

Turn out onto a floured work surface and knead *only* until the dough is no longer sticky. Place the dough in a lightly greased bowl and very lightly grease the surface.

Allow the dough to rise for 20 minutes. Punch down, allow the dough to rise again for 20 minutes. Punch down and shape as desired.

NOTE: Whole wheat flour may be used in place of white flour. Do not overknead.

Makes 2-3 loaves or 4 dozen buns.

KUGELHOPF

15 mL	active dry yeast	1 tbsp.
5 mL	sugar	1 tsp.
50 mL	warm water	¼ cup
175 mL	butter or margarine	¾ cup
125 mL	sugar	½ cup
4	eggs	4
175 mL	milk, scalded	¾ cup
1 L	sifted flour	4 cups
5 mL	salt	1 tsp.
250 mL	golden raisins	1 cup
125 mL	slivered almonds	½ cup
15 mL	grated lemon rind	1 tbsp.
125 mL	finely chopped almonds	½ cup

In a small bowl, dissolve yeast and 5 mL (1 tsp.) sugar in warm water. In a large bowl cream butter and sugar until light; add the eggs one at a time, beating after each addition. Scald milk and cool to lukewarm. Add milk and 500 mL (2 cups) of the flour to the egg mixture. Add the yeast mixture and beat until well blended. Add remaining flour and salt; beat until batter is smooth. Stir in raisins, almonds and lemon rind.

Grease a large kugelhopf mold or 2.5 L (10 cup) mold and sprinkle with the chopped almonds, turning pan so the bottom and sides will be covered.

For an airy, coarse-textured coffee-bread, turn the batter immediately into the greased mold and let rise as directed below. For a fine textured coffee-bread, cover bowl lightly and let rise in a warm place until doubled, about 2 hours. Beat batter down and turn into the greased mold to rise. Let rise in warm place until batter comes to about 6 mm (¼") of the top of the mold. If you use a traditional kugelhopf mold or another 2.5 L (10 cup) mold with tube, bake in moderately hot oven 190°C (375°F) 45-50 minutes. If you use a 2.5 L (10 cup) tubeless mold bake at 180°C (350°F) for 60-65 minutes. Bake until cake tester comes out clean. Let cool in pan; turn out. Serves 12-16.

JALAPENO-CHEESE BUNS

½ recipe sweet dough (refer to recipe 36)		
250 mL	mozzarella cheese	1 cup
250 mL	old cheddar cheese	1 cup
50-125 mL	chopped pickled jalapeno peppers	¼-½ cup
50-125 mL	flour	¼-½ cup
	Grease two 1 L (9"x1 ¼") pie plates	

Let dough rise and punch down. Knead both cheeses and jalapeno peppers into dough. Work in some flour if dough becomes sticky. Allow dough to rest 15 minutes. Punch down. Shape into buns. Place into prepared pans and allow to rise until almost double in bulk.

Oven Method:

Bake at 200°C (400°F) for 10 minutes, reduce heat to 190°C (375°F). Continue baking 35-40 minutes.

Barbecue Method:

(Dual Control)

Preheat barbecue on high with lid down for 10 minutes. Place buns on grid, towards one side. Turn heat off directly under buns. Close lid. Baking time will depend on the outdoor temperature and wind. Approximate times, 40-65 minutes. Buns may need to be rotated to prevent burning.

Makes 2 dozen.

39

PUMPERNICKEL BRIE WREATH

15 mL	yeast	1 tbsp.
300 mL	warm water, 43 C (110 F)	1 ¼ cups
50 mL	molasses	¼ cup
5 mL	salt	1 tsp.
30 mL	butter, melted and cooled	2 tbsps.
1	egg, separated	1
50 mL	unsweetened cocoa	¼ cup
15 mL	caraway seeds	1 tbsp.
500 mL	all purpose flour	2 cups
375-500 mL	rye flour	1 ½-2 cups
1-20 cm	round Brie cheese	1-8"
	Red grapes for garnish	

In a large bowl of an electric mixer, sprinkle yeast over warm water, let stand for 5 minutes to soften.

Stir in 250 mL (1 cup) all-purpose flour using electric mixer. Stir in molasses, salt, butter, egg yolk, cocoa and caraway seeds. Then stir in remaining all-purpose flour, scraping bowl often.

Beat at medium speed for 8 minutes. With a heavy duty mixer or wooden spoon, beat in rye flour, 50 mL (¼ cup) at a time, until dough is smooth and pulls cleanly away from bowl.

Turn out onto a floured board and knead until elastic and smooth (about 5 minutes), adding more rye flour as needed to prevent sticking.

Place dough in a greased bowl; turn to grease top. Cover and let rise in a warm place until doubled (about 1½ hours).

Generously grease the outside of a 20 cm (8") round cake pan and set in the center of a well greased 35 cm x 40 cm (14" x 17") baking sheet or 40 cm (17") round pizza pan. Punch dough down; turn out and knead on a lightly floured board until smooth.

Divide into 3 equal portions. Roll each piece, one at a time (keeping others covered) into a smooth 90 cm (36") long strand. Braid the three strands together and wrap around greased cake pan. Join ends, pinch to seal.

Cover and let rise in a warm place until almost doubled. Lightly brush braid with beaten egg white.

Bake in 180°C (350°F) oven for 40 minutes or until well browned. Use a knife to loosen bread around pan, then lift out pan. Using a spatula, slide bread onto a large wire rack. Let cool.

Bread can be frozen when thoroughly cooled, for up to 1 month. To serve, place wreath on a large bread board. Cut a small section into 6 mm (¼") slices, then place Brie in centre, spreading wreath if necessary, setting slices back in place. Garnish with grapes.

Makes 15 to 18 servings.

STICKY CINNAMON KNOTS

Sticky Syrup:

125 mL	brown sugar	½ cup
50 mL	margarine or butter	¼ cup
15 mL	corn syrup	1 tbsp.

Knots:

½	recipe sweet dough (refer to recipe 36)	½
250 mL	margarine or butter	1 cup
250 mL	white sugar	1 cup
250 mL	brown sugar	1 cup
30 mL	cinnamon	2 tbsps.

Combine the ingredients for sticky syrup and heat slowly. Pour the syrup in bottom of a 3.5 L (9″ x 13″ x 2″) pan. Set aside.

Turn raised sweet dough onto a lightly floured table. Roll out to form a 35 x 50 cm (14″ x 20″) rectangle, 1 cm (½″) thick. Cut into approximately 7.5 or 10 cm (3″ or 4″) square pieces.

Dip each piece first into melted margarine, then coat well with the white and brown sugar-cinnamon mixture.

Stretch the dough piece and form into a simple knot. Place knots side by side in the prepared pan. Let buns rise until almost double. Bake at 180° C (350° F) for 30 to 40 minutes.

Makes 12-15 knots.

COCONUT BUNS

41

½	recipe sweet dough *(refer to recipe 36)*	½

Coconut filling

200 g	unsweetened medium coconut	7 oz.
175 mL	sugar	¾ cup
125 mL	melted butter	½ cup
1	egg, beaten	1

Combine ingredients for coconut filling. Set aside.

Dust risen dough with a little flour then roll into a 30 x 45 cm (12″ x 18″) rectangle keeping the sides straight. Brush rectangle with beaten egg and spread with coconut filling leaving one long edge free of filling.

Roll up jelly roll fashion toward uncoated edge. Seal.

Cut into slices about 2 cm (¾″) thick. Place on flattened greased paper muffin cups on baking sheet.

Allow to rise for 50 minutes, covered with a towel. Brush with egg then bake in preheated 180° C (350° F) oven for 10 to 15 minutes.

Remove to cooling rack and brush with a sugar-water solution: 30 mL (2 tbsps.) sugar and 15 mL (1 tbsp.) water.

Makes 24 buns.

ORANGE BUBBLE BREAD

250 mL	skim milk, scalded*	1 cup
10 mL	sugar	2 tsps.
15 mL	yeast	1 tbsp.
875 mL	flour	3 ½ cups
5 mL	salt	1 tsp.
50 mL	sugar	¼ cup
125 mL	chilled butter	½ cup
2	eggs, beaten	2
250 mL	sugar	1 cup
20 mL	grated orange rind	4 tsps.
250 mL	toasted desiccated coconut	1 cup
125 mL	melted butter	½ cup
50-125 mL raisins		¼-½ cup

*Or use 250 mL (1 cup) warm water and add 75 mL (⅓ cup) skim milk powder to flour.

Scald milk and cool to lukewarm (or use lukewarm water). Add the 10 mL (2 tsps.) sugar and yeast; stir together the flour, salt, and 50 mL (¼ cup) sugar. (If using skim milk powder, add here). Cut the butter into the sifted dry ingredients until size of split peas. Combine 250 mL (1 cup) of the flour mixture with yeast, add beaten eggs. Add to dry ingredients. *Mix thoroughly.* Turn out onto lightly floured board and knead until smooth, adding additional flour gradually, if required, until dough is no longer sticky. Place into well-greased bowl, turning dough to grease surface.

Cover and allow to rise until double in warm draft-free place. While dough is rising, combine the 250 mL (1 cup) sugar, grated rind and coconut. Rub mixture well between the hands to

release orange oil into the sugar. Prepare pan. Grease bottom and sides of large angel food cake pan and sprinkle 45 mL (3 tbsps.) of coconut-sugar mixture over the base. When dough is risen, punch down and cut into 2.5 cm (1 inch) pieces. Roll into balls; dip into cooled, melted butter and then into coconut-sugar mixture, coating each ball completely. Arrange in layers, with a few raisins between. Sprinkle with 30 mL (2 tbsps.) sugar mixture and drizzle with remaining melted butter.

Cover and allow to rise until double in bulk. Bake at 190° C (375° F) for 50 minutes. If the bread becomes dark before it is baked, cover loosely with a piece of aluminum foil. Remove from oven and invert immediately onto cake rack.

NOTE: If using pan with removable bottom, cover outside of pan completely with aluminum foil - dull side out to prevent butter from dripping into oven. Variation: Use lemon rind in place of grated orange rind.

CRUNCHY HEALTH BREAD

625 mL	scalded milk	2 ½ cups
250 mL	wheat germ	1 cup
250 mL	Roman Meal or other coarse dry cereal*	1 cup
375 mL	warm water 43° C (110°F)	1 ½ cups
30 mL	dark brown sugar	2 tbsps.
30 mL	dry yeast	2 tbsps.
125 mL	molasses or honey	½ cup
125 mL	oil	½ cup
125 mL	sesame seeds	½ cup
20 mL	salt	4 tsps.
750 mL	whole wheat flour	3 cups
1.25 L	unsifted all-purpose flour	5 cups

(SunnyBoy or Red River Cereal)

Scald milk. Pour scalded milk over wheat germ and Roman Meal to soften in large mixing bowl. Stir and let cool to lukewarm. Meanwhile, dissolve yeast and dark brown sugar in warm water. To cooled cereal mixture, add molasses, oil, seeds and salt. Beat in whole wheat flour, then dissolved yeast. Work in enough all-purpose flour to form a soft but not sticky dough. Knead on a floured board just until smooth and elastic. Form dough into 3 loaves and place in well-greased 21.5 cm x 4 cm (8½" x 4½") loaf pans. Cover and let rise in a warm place, free from drafts, until double in bulk (about 1-1½ hours). Bake at 190°C (375°F) for 20 minutes, reduce the heat to 180°C (350°F) and bake an additional 20 minutes or until loaves sound hollow when tapped. Makes 3 loaves.

NOTE: Too much kneading will cause dough to become sticky again.

Favorite Desserts

PEACH FLAN

	pastry for a 25 cm (10″) flan	
125 mL	flour	½ cup
125 mL	sugar	½ cup
375 mL	milk	1 ½ cups
3	egg yolks	3
125 mL	butter	½ cup
45 mL	almond-flavoured liqueur	3 tbsps.
7 mL	vanilla	1 ½ tsps.
50 mL	slivered almonds	¼ cup
125 g	green seedless grapes, cut in half	¼ lb.
5	peaches, peeled & halved	5
2	strawberries, cut in half	2
175 mL	apricot jam	¾ cup
7 mL	almond-flavoured liqueur	1 ½ tsps.
	Preheat oven to 190° C (375° F)	

Roll out pastry and line a 25 cm (10″) flan pan. Lightly prick the bottom and sides with a fork. Bake in preheated oven for 12 to 15 minutes or until lightly browned.

Remove and leave at room temperature to cool. Measure flour and sugar into a heavy-bottomed saucepan. Gradually whisk in milk, then place over medium heat. Stir constantly until the mixture comes to a boil. Continue to stir or whisk until it is very thick. Remove from heat. Beat egg yolks together and gradually blend a little of the hot mixture into egg yolks. Then whisk the egg yolks into the hot mixture and continue to whisk until well mixed. Add butter, liqueur and vanilla and stir until the butter is melted. Stir in the almonds. Pour into baked flan shell and spread until smooth. Cool.

Place grapes around edge of flan, reserving 8 halves for centre. Then arrange peach halves in a circular fashion, placing 1 half in centre. Surround with remaining grapes and strawberries.

Prepare glaze by heating apricot jam with remaining liqueur in a heavy-bottomed saucepan. Heat until jam is melted, then strain into a bowl. Spoon over fruit. Refrigerate until ready to serve. Serves 10-12.

45

FROSTED MERINGUE WITH KIWIS

3	egg whites	3
1 mL	cream of tartar	¼ tsp.
2 mL	vanilla	½ tsp.
175 mL	sugar	¾ cup
250 mL	chilled whipping cream	1 cup
30 mL	sugar	2 tbsps.
3	*kiwis, peeled and slivered	3

*Note: 2 cups of fresh strawberries, halved; raspberries or blueberries may be substituted for the kiwis.

Preheat oven to 110°C (225°F). Place a 25 cm (10″) round piece of cooking parchment or greased brown paper on baking sheet.

Beat egg whites and cream of tartar until foamy; add vanilla. Beat in 175 mL (¾ cup) sugar, a small amount at a time. Continue beating until stiff and glossy. Spread on paper.

Bake 2 hours. Turn off oven and leave meringue in oven with door closed until cool. Remove from paper.

Beat whipping cream and 30 mL (2 tbsps.) sugar in chilled bowl until stiff. Frost sides and top of meringue, building up top edge slightly. Let soften in refrigerator 2-3 hours. Arrange kiwi slices on top. Cut into wedges to serve.

Serves 8.

IMPERIAL RICE WITH CREPE RUFFLES

125 mL	uncooked regular long-grained rice	½ cup
500 mL	light cream	2 cups
75 mL	sugar	⅓ cup
3	egg yolks	3
2 mL	vanilla	½ tsp.
250 mL	heavy cream	1 cup
50 mL	sugar	¼ cup
50 mL	boiling water	3 tbsps.
50 mL	shelled hazelnuts, toasted, skinned and halved	¼ cup
50 mL	diced and mixed candied fruit	¼ cup

Crepe Ruffles

2	eggs	2
125 mL	flour	½ cup
125 mL	milk	½ cup
30 mL	water	2 tbsps.
15 mL	butter or margarine, melted	1 tbsp.
	vegetable oil (for frying)	

Parboil rice in water in a large saucepan for 5 minutes. Drain; return to pan. Add light cream and 75 mL (⅓ cup) sugar; cover. Cook on low heat, stirring occasionally, for 40 minutes or until rice is tender but not mushy and cream is absorbed. Beat yolks in cup; stir spoonful of hot rice into yolks; stir yolk mixture into rice in pan. Cook 1 minute; remove from heat. Stir in vanilla and heavy cream. Cover surface of pudding with plastic wrap; chill until cold.

Heat 50 mL (¼ cup) sugar in a small heavy saucepan until melted and golden; stir in boiling water until smooth and sizzling stops. Stir in nuts and fruit; cool slightly. (If sauce hardens, reheat until spoonable). Spoon pudding into glass bowl. Arrange about 6 to 10 Crepe Ruffles on top (how many depends on diameter of bowl); drizzle with caramel sauce.

Combine eggs, flour, milk, water and butter. Blend until smooth. Chill at least 2 hours or overnight. Using 30 mL (2 tbsps.) batter for each crepe; fry in hot greased 15 cm (6-7″) skillet, tilting pan to make a very thin crepe; when light brown, turn to brown other side. (These can be made ahead and frozen, if you wish). Fill medium-sized saucepan with 1.2 cm (½″) oil. Heat to 190°C (350°F) on a deep fat thermometer. Fold each crepe in half; roll into cone. Lower cones one at a time, into oil, holding with tongs until shape is maintained. Fry 3 or 4 at a time, turning once, until golden. Drain on paper towelling. Store in airtight container if made ahead.

Serves 6-8.

BLACK FOREST SOUFFLE

500 mL	frozen sour pitted cherries, thawed, quartered	2 cups
80 mL	kirsch, or cherry flavoured liqueur	6 tbsps.
2	envelopes unflavoured gelatin	2
175 mL	sugar	¾ cup
3	eggs, separated	3
500 mL	milk	2 cups
4	squares semi-sweet chocolate	4
7 mL	vanilla	1 ½ tsps.
500 mL	whipping cream, unwhipped	2 cups
	chocolate curls for garnish	

Marinate cherries in 30 mL (2 tbsps.) kirsch. In a medium saucepan, mix unflavoured gelatin with 125 mL (½ cup) sugar. Beat egg yolks with milk and add to gelatin mixture with chocolate squares. Stir over low heat until gelatin is completely dissolved and chocolate melts. Remove from heat.

Add remaining 50 mL (¼ cup) kirsch and vanilla. With a wire whisk, beat mixture until chocolate is well blended. Chill, stirring occasionally, until mixture mounds slightly when dropped from a spoon. In a large bowl, beat egg whites until soft peaks form; gradually add remaining 50 mL (¼ cup) sugar and beat until stiff. Fold in gelatin mixture. In a medium bowl, whip 425 mL (1¾ cups) whipping cream and fold into gelatin mixture with chopped cherries and kirsch. Turn into a 1 L (1 qt.) souffle dish with a 7.5 cm (3″) collar. Chill until set, about 4 hours. Remove collar. Top with remaining whipping cream, whipped, and chocolate curls.

Serves 12.

PUMPKIN CHEESECAKE

1	ginger-graham crust *(recipe follows)*	1
3 x 250 g	cream cheese	3 x 8 oz.
250 mL	light brown sugar	1 cup
125 mL	granulated sugar	½ cup
5	eggs	5
450 g	canned pumpkin puree	16 oz.
5 mL	cinnamon	1 tsp.
1 mL	ground nutmeg	¼ tsp.
1 mL	ground cloves	¼ tsp.
50 mL	heavy cream	¼ cup
5 mL	vanilla	1 tsp.

Using an electric mixer, beat the cream cheese until smoooth at medium speed. Add sugars gradually. Add eggs, one at a time, beating well after each addition. Beat in pumpkin, spices, heavy cream and vanilla at lower speed.

Pour into a buttered 22 cm (9″) springform pan lined with ginger-graham crust.

Bake in a 160°C (325°F) oven for 1 hour and 35 minutes. Turn off oven and allow cheesecake to remain in oven with door closed for 30 minutes longer.

Remove cake from the oven. Cool on a wire rack. Chill several hours or overnight.

Serves 12.

Ginger Graham Crust:

125 mL	graham cracker crumbs	½ cup
125 mL	crushed ginger snaps	½ cup
50 mL	granulated sugar	¼ cup
50 mL	melted butter	¼ cup

Combine ingredients well and line bottom of a buttered 22 cm (9″) springform pan.

Chill briefly before filling.

49

RASPBERRY MANDARIN ORANGE TRIFLE

Cake

6	large eggs	6
250 mL	sugar	1 cup
250 mL	flour	1 cup
75 mL	melted clarified butter	⅓ cup
5 mL	vanilla	1 tsp.
4 mL	orange rind or tangerine rind	¾ tsp.

Filling

150 mL	strained raspberry jam	⅔ cup
3-300 g	frozen raspberries, thawed	3 - 10 oz.
125 mL	orange or tangerine juice	½ cup
50 mL	orange-flavoured liqueur	3 tbsps.
2-284 mL	canned mandarin orange sections, drained	2 - 10 oz.

Custard Sauce

9	large egg yolks	9
125 mL	sugar	½ cup
	Pinch salt	
5 mL	grated orange or tangerine rind	1 tsp.
425 mL	milk	1¾ cups
375 mL	half and half cream	1½ cups
25 mL	cornstarch	1½ tbsps.

Make the cake:
Preheat oven to 180°C (350°F). Line the bottoms of two 1.5 L (9″) round cake pans with wax paper and dust pans with flour, shaking out excess.

In a bowl with an electric mixer beat eggs and sugar until mixture is well combined. Set bowl over a saucepan containing 5 cm (2″) of hot but not boiling water and heat mixture over low heat, stirring occasionally until mixture is lukewarm. Remove bowl from pan and beat mixture at high speed until it is very light and triple in volume. Sift in flour one third at a time, folding thoroughly and gently. Fold in butter 15 mL (1 tbsp.) at a time. Fold in vanilla and rind. Pour batter evenly, into 2 pans.

Bake 20 to 25 minutes or until cake tester inserted in center comes out clean. Allow cakes to cool in pan on a rack for 10 minutes, then remove from pans; remove wax paper and cool completely.

Prepare the custard:

In a bowl with an electric beater beat yolks with sugar, rind and a pinch of salt until mixture ribbons when beater is lifted.

In a large heavy saucepan combine milk, cream and cornstarch. Bring liquid to a simmer stirring constantly. Add liquid to yolk mixture in a stream, stirring constantly; transfer custard to saucepan and cook it over moderate heat stirring constantly until it is thickened, do not allow it to boil.

Strain custard into a metal bowl set in a bowl of cracked ice and let it cool, stirring occasionally. If not using the sauce immediately, let it stand covered with a buttered round of waxed paper, at room temperature for up to 1 hour.

To assemble the trifle: Drain 2 packages of the raspberries well. Cut each cake in half horizontally to form 4 layers. Spread the cut side of 2 layers with the jam. Place one layer, jam-side up, into a deep glass serving bowl 9 inches in diameter.

Spoon half the drained raspberries around the outside edge of this layer. Put ¼ of the custard into the centre and spread to cover.

Sprinkle the cut side of one of the plain layers with half the orange juice mixed with the liqueur. Place this layer cut-side down over the raspberry layer in the bowl.

Arrange half the mandarin orange sections decoratively around the edge. Add another ¼ of the custard and spread to cover. Repeat with the remaining jam and plain layers as before.

Drain the remaining package of raspberries reserving the juice. In a food processor or blender puree the raspberries with 50 mL (¼ cup) of the reserved juice. Strain the puree through a fine sieve into a pitcher. Beginning in the center of the trifle

drizzle the puree in a spiral pattern over the sauce and with the tip of a knife retrace the spiral to smooth the line. Beginning each time at the center draw the tip of the knife lightly through the spiral to the edge in 4 straight lines at right angles to each other to form a cross, wiping the blade each time. Reverse the process from the edge to the center, dividing each quarter into half again. Chill the trifle, covered, for a least 4 hours or overnight.

Allow to stand at room temperature for 1 hour before serving. Serves 10-12.

CANTALOUPE SORBET

125 mL	sugar	½ cup
50 mL	light corn syrup	¼ cup
175 mL	water	¾ cup
1	large ripe cantaloupe	1
15 mL	lemon juice	1 tbsp.
125 mL	anisette liqueur	½ cup

In a small saucepan, combine sugar, corn syrup and water. Stir over low heat until sugar dissolves, cool to room temperature. Cut cantaloupe from rind; remove and discard seeds. Puree cantaloupe and lemon juice in blender or food processor until smooth. In a medium bowl, combine puree, cooled syrup and anisette. Pour into ice cream canister and freeze in ice cream maker according to manufacturer's directions or pour prepared mixture into a 9 inch square pan or several undivided ice trays. Cover with foil or plastic wrap. Place in freezer, freeze until firm, 3-6 hours.

Scrape frozen mixture with a fork or spoon until pieces resemble finely crushed ice. Serve immediately.

For a smoother texture, freeze prepared mixture until firm; break into small pieces. Spoon half of frozen mixture into chilled food processor bowl. Beat with metal blade until light and fluffy but not thawed. Repeat with remaining frozen mixture. Serve immediately or return beaten mixture to pan and freeze until firm, 1-3 hours.

Makes 1 L (1 qt.)

RHUBARB COBBLER

Sauce:

500 mL	diced rhubarb	2 cups
15 mL	flour	1 tbsp.
150 mL	honey	⅔ cup
5 mL	grated orange rind	1 tsp.
5 mL	cinnamon	1 tsp.

Batter:

250 mL	flour	1 cup
10 mL	baking powder	2 tsps.
2 mL	salt	½ tsp.
50 mL	shortening	¼ cup
1	egg, beaten	1
45 mL	milk	3 tbsps.
30 mL	honey	2 tbsps.
	light cream (optional)	
	Preheat oven to 180° C (350°F)	

Sauce: Combine ingredients for sauce; pour in a well greased 2 L (8″ x 8″) baking pan.

Batter: Combine flour, baking powder and salt. Cut in shortening. Mix egg, milk, and honey. Add to flour-shortening mixture and stir only until dry ingredients are moistened. (Batter will be stiff).

Drop by spoonfuls on rhubarb, spread. Bake for 35 minutes or until golden brown. Serve warm with cream if desired.

Serves 6.

APPLE-RING WITH EGGNOG SAUCE

14	red Delicious apples	14
2 mL	ascorbic acid	½ tsp.
175 mL	flour	¾ cup
125 mL	honey	½ cup
90 mL	well-chilled unsalted butter	6 tbsps.
50 mL	frozen apple juice concentrate	¼ cup
30 mL	honey	2 tbsps.
	Eggnog Sauce (recipe follows)	

Peel (optional) and core apples [may be refrigerated overnight in water with Vitamin C (ascorbic acid) added].

Preheat oven to 190°C (375°F). Slice apples with sharp knife into 5 mm (¼ inch) slices. Cream honey and butter and add flour to make crumbs. Dip apple slices into crumb mixture and set them side by side around the edge of a 25 cm (10″) quiche dish or pie plate, filling gaps with half slices to make a tight ring. Mound the remaining slices in the center, and sprinkle with remaining crumb mixture. Bake 30 minutes. Reduce heat to 180°C (350°F) and bake 20-30 minutes more or until topping is lightly browned.

Heat frozen apple juice concentrate and 30 mL (2 tbsps.) honey in a small saucepan, pour over warm apple-ring. Serve with Eggnog Sauce.

Eggnog Sauce:

4	large egg yolks	4
30 mL	honey	2 tbsps.
50 mL	frozen apple juice concentrate	4 tbsps.
4 mL	freshly grated nutmeg	¾ tsp.
2 mL	vanilla	½ tsp.
250 mL	whipping cream or evaporated milk	1 cup

Cream egg yolks and honey. Add apple juice concentrate, nutmeg, vanilla and cream. Simmer on top of stove until thickened, about 5 minutes. Serves 8-12.

ANGEL LEMON DELIGHT

1	angel food cake, purchased, homemade or from a mix	1

Filling:

10	egg yolks	10
150 mL	sugar	⅔ cup
150 mL	freshly squeezed lemon juice	⅔ cup
125 mL	butter at room temperature	½ cup
10 mL	grated lemon rind	2 tsps.
250 mL	whipping cream	1 cup

Icing:

625 mL	whipping cream	2½ cups
75 mL	icing sugar	⅓ cup
5 mL	lemon rind	1 tsp.
	lemon slices	
	grated lemon rind	
	sugared lemon candies	

To make filling: whisk together egg yolks, sugar and lemon juice thoroughly in small heavy saucepan. Cook over low heat, stirring constantly until mixture is very thick, about 5 minutes. Do not allow mixture to boil or it will curdle. Remove from heat; whisk in butter, 5 mL (1 tsp.) at a time, until thoroughly incorporated. Stir in lemon rind. Scrape filling into small bowl.

Cover surface of filling with greased wax paper to prevent skin from forming. Refrigerate until cold, about 1 hour. Whip 250 mL (1 cup) cream. Fold into cooled lemon mixture and set aside. Cut 2.5 cm (1″) layer from top of cake. Leaving a 1.2 cm (½″) edge inside and outside, scoop out cake to make a tunnel. Fill tunnel with prepared lemon filling up to top of cake. Replace removed layer.

To make icing: Whip cream until it begins to thicken. Add icing sugar and lemon rind and continue beating until stiff. Frost top and sides of cake with icing. Decorate with lemon slices and lemon rind or sugared lemon candies. Refrigerate cake overnight before serving. Serves 8-12.

Favorite Cakes

MARASCHINO CHOCOLATE CAKE

150 mL	shortening	⅔ cup
325 mL	sugar	1 ½ cups
2	eggs	2
2 squares	unsweetened chocolate, melted	2 squares
125 mL	maraschino cherries, chopped	½ cup
750 mL	cake flour	3 cups
10 mL	soda	2 tsp.
1 mL	salt	¼ tsp.
50 mL	maraschino cherry juice	¼ cup
425 mL	sour milk or buttermilk	1 ¾ cups
	Preheat oven to 180° C (350°F)	

Line three 1.5 L (9″) layer cake pans with wax paper. Combine shortening and sugar, cream thoroughly. Beat in eggs one at a time. Add cooled melted chocolate and cherries. Sift flour and measure. Resift with soda and salt.

Add cherry juice to milk. Add to the cake mixture alternately with flour beginning and ending with dry ingredients.

Pour into prepared pans. Bake 50-55 minutes or until top springs back when lightly pressed by finger. Cool in pans for 5 minutes. Remove from pans and finish cooling. When fully cooled, fill and frost with Chantilly Cream. Serves 16-20.

Chantilly Whipped Cream

125 mL	whipping cream	½ cup
30 mL	icing sugar	2 tbsps.
30 mL	cherry liqueur or maraschino juice	2 tbsps.
1-2 drops	red food colouring	1-2 drops

Beat all ingredients at high speed until stiff peaks form.

POPPY SEED LEMON LOAF

4	eggs	4
375 mL	oil	1½ cups
375 mL	light cream	1½ cups
5 mL	vanilla	1 tsp.
125 mL	poppy seeds	½ cup
750 mL	flour	3 cups
500 mL	sugar	2 cups
5 mL	salt	1 tsp.
7 mL	baking soda	1½ tsps.
10 mL	baking powder	2 tsps.
1	grated rind and juice of lemon	1
50 mL	sugar	¼ cup

Preheat oven to 160°C (325°F). Combine eggs, oil, cream, vanilla and poppy seeds. Mix together flour, sugar, salt, baking soda, baking powder and lemon rind.

Add dry ingredients to the egg-cream mixture and blend well. Pour into 2 well greased 2 L (9"x 4"x 3") loaf pans or 18 muffin tins. Bake the loaves for 70 minutes or the muffins for 30-35 minutes.

Meanwhile, mix the lemon juice with the 50 mL (¼ cup) sugar. Pour over the bread or muffins while they are still hot in the pan.

Yield: 2 loaves or 18 large muffins.

SPICED PUMPKIN ROLL

175 mL	flour	¾ cup
10 mL	ground cinnamon	2 tsps.
5 mL	baking powder	1 tsp.
5 mL	ground ginger	1 tsp.
2 mL	ground nutmeg	½ tsp.
2 mL	salt	½ tsp.
3	eggs	3
250 mL	sugar	1 cup
150 mL	canned pumpkin	⅔ cup
5 mL	vanilla	1 tsp.
1 L	ice cream (almond or vanilla), softened	1 qt.

Preheat oven to 190°C (375°F). Line a 2 L (10"x15") greased jellyroll pan with waxed paper. Mix flour, cinnamon, baking powder, ginger, nutmeg and salt; set aside. In a mixer bowl, beat eggs at high speed for 5 minutes or until thick; gradually beat in granulated sugar. Using low speed, mix in pumpkin, vanilla and the flour mixture.

Spread batter in prepared pan. Bake 15 minutes or until top springs back when touched. Immediately invert cake onto a paper towel sprinkled with icing sugar. Remove wax paper; beginning at short edge roll cake and towel together, jelly-roll fashion. Cool completely.

Unroll cake, spread with ice cream, and reroll. Wrap and freeze. Before serving, let stand at room temperature 10-15 minutes; dust with powdered sugar.

Serves 8-10.

DATE CAKE

250 mL	boiling water	1 cup
250 mL	dates	1 cup
5 mL	baking soda	1 tsp.
125 mL	butter	½ cup
250 mL	sugar	1 cup
1	egg	1
375 mL	flour	1 ½ cups
2 mL	salt	½ tsp.
5 mL	vanilla	1 tsp.

Preheat oven to 180°C (350°F). Grease a 3 L (8"x12") pan. Pour boiling water over dates and soda. Let stand while mixing batter. Combine butter and sugar, cream well. Add egg and beat until light and fluffy. Add flour and salt alternately with cooled date mixture. Add vanilla. Pour into prepared pan. Bake 45 mins. While cake is baking mix together the following:

50 mL	melted butter	¼ cup
125 mL	brown sugar	½ cup
30 mL	milk	2 tbsps.
250 mL	walnuts, chopped	1 cup

Remove cake from oven, spread with nut mixture. Place under broiler and broil until light brown. (Watch carefully — burns quickly. Use bottom of broiler — no rack.) Serves 12.

RASPBERRY PECAN TORTE

Torte:

425 mL	flour	1 ¾ cups
10 mL	baking powder	2 tsps.
2 mL	salt	½ tsp.
250 mL	ground pecans	1 cup
375 mL	whipping cream	1 ½ cups
375 mL	sugar	1 ½ cups
15 mL	vanilla	3 tsps.
3	eggs	3

Frosting:

375 mL	whipping cream, unwhipped	1 ½ cups
225 g	cream cheese, softened	8 oz.
250 mL	sugar	1 cup
5 mL	vanilla	1 tsp.
500 mL	raspberry jam, sieved	2 cups

Torte: Preheat oven to 180°C (350°F). Grease and flour two 1.5 L (9″) round cake pans. Combine flour, baking powder, salt and ground pecans. Set aside. Beat cream until stiff peaks form. Set aside. In a large bowl combine sugar, vanilla and eggs; beat 5 minutes on high. Fold dry ingredients and whipped cream alternately into egg mixture. Pour batter into prepared pans.

Bake 25 minutes or until toothpick inserted in center comes out clean. Cool 15 minutes; remove from pans. Cool completely.

Frosting:
Beat whipping cream until stiff peaks form. In a separate bowl combine cream cheese, sugar and vanilla. Blend well. Fold in whipped cream.

To assemble torte:
Split each layer in half horizontally to form 4 layers. Place one layer on serving plate; spread with 125 mL (½ cup) frosting. Top with second layer; spread with 250 mL (1 cup) raspberry jam. Top with third cake layer; spread with 125 mL (½ cup) frosting. Top with remaining cake layer. Frost sides of cake with frosting, reserving about 250 mL (1 cup) for decorating. Spread remaining jam on top of cake. Using a pastry bag and star tip, pipe reserved frosting in lattice design over top of cake; pipe border around top and bottom edges. Store in refrigerator.

Serves 16-20.

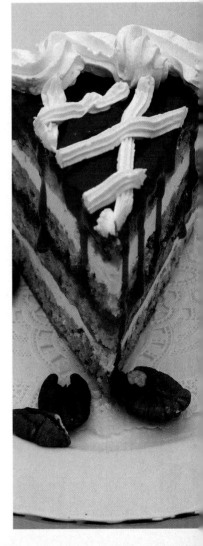

ORANGE MOCHA GATEAU

1 (520 g)	orange cake mix	1 (520 g)
125 mL	orange flavoured liqueur	½ cup

Mousse Filling:

4	large eggs	4
125 mL	sugar	½ cup
1 pkg.	unflavoured gelatin	1 pkg.
50 mL	orange juice	¼ cup
3	squares semi-sweet chocolate	3
3	squares unsweetened chocolate	3
45 mL	instant coffee powder	3 tbsps.
50 mL	orange flavoured liqueur	¼ cup
15 mL	grated orange rind	1 tbsp.
250 mL	whipping cream	1 cup

Orange Mocha Icing:

30 mL	instant coffee	2 tbsps.
30 mL	hot water	2 tbsps.
30 mL	orange liqueur	2 tbsps.
75 mL	cocoa powder	5 tbsps.
125 mL	butter (room temperature)	½ cup
225 g	cream cheese (room temperature)	4 oz.
1 L	icing sugar	4 cups
12	candied expresso coffee beans	12

The day before serving the cake, prepare your favourite orange cake mix in 2-1.5 L (9″) round cake pans. Allow the cakes to cool thoroughly.

Prepare Mousse Filling:
Separate eggs while cold; yolks into a small bowl, whites into large. Blend sugar into yolks. In another small bowl, dissolve gelatin in orange juice. Place chocolate, instant coffee and orange liqueur in the top of a double boiler. Melt over hot (not boiling) water. When chocolate is melted and smooth, stir in orange rind. Remove from heat. Beat egg yolk-sugar mixture until light and fluffy. Stir into chocolate mixture, then stir in softened gelatin. Return pot over hot water and cook for

4-5 minutes. Remove from heat and cool to room temperature. Beat egg whites until stiff but not dry and gently fold into cooled chocolate mixture. Whip cream until stiff and fold into mixture. Cover and set aside.

Assemble Cake:
Cut each layer in half horizontally, forming 4 layers. Drizzle 30 mL (2 tbsps.) liqueur evenly over the cut sides of each layer (125 mL/½ cup total). Allow to stand 10 minutes. Place one layer cut-side up on cake plate. Spread with ⅓ cup of the mousse filling. Cover with second layer and more mousse. Repeat. Top with fourth layer cut-side down. Cover the cake well and refrigerate overnight to set the filling.

Prepare frosting:
The day of serving, in a small bowl dissolve the coffee in the hot water. Stir in the liqueur. Add cocoa, butter and cream cheese and beat until blended. Add icing sugar gradually, beating until smooth and creamy. Frost top and sides of cake. Garnish with candied coffee beans. Refrigerate to firm the icing.

Serves 12.

HAZELNUT TORTE

6	eggs, separated	6
175 mL	sugar	¾ cup
75 mL	fine dry bread crumbs	⅓ cup
50 mL	flour	¼ cup
250 mL	ground hazelnuts	1 cup
500 mL	whipping cream	2 cups
10 mL	vanilla	2 tsps.
50 mL	icing sugar	¼ cup

Preheat oven to 160°C (325°F). In a large bowl, beat egg whites until soft peaks form. Gradually sprinkle 50 mL (¼ cup) sugar into egg whites beating well. Whites should stand in stiff peaks. In a small bowl, beat egg yolks until thick and lemon-coloured. Gradually beat in 125 mL (½ cup) sugar until blended. Stir in bread crumbs, flour and 150 mL (⅔ cup) ground nuts. With a wire whisk or rubber spatula, fold into beaten egg whites. Pour batter into a 3 L (9″) springform pan and spread evenly.

Bake 50-60 minutes or until cake springs back when lightly touched with finger. Invert cake in pan on wire rack, cool completely.

In a small bowl, beat whipping cream, vanilla, and icing sugar until stiff peaks form. Remove cake from pan. With a long sharp knife slice cake horizontally into two layers. Place bottom layer on cake platter; spread with ¼ whipped cream mixture; top with second layer. Frost sides of cake with half of remaining whipped cream mixture. With hand gently press remaining 75 mL (⅓ cup) ground nuts onto cream. Spoon remaining whipped cream mixture into a pastry bag with a large rosette tube; use to decorate top of cake.

Serves 12-14.

BURNT SUGAR CHIFFON CAKE

250 mL	sugar	1 cup
125 mL	boiling water	½ cup
550 mL	cake flour	2¼ cups
300 mL	sugar	1¼ cups
15 mL	baking powder	1 tbsp.
5 mL	salt	1 tsp.
125 mL	salad oil	½ cup
5	unbeaten egg yolks	5
90 mL	cold water	6 tbsps.
5 mL	vanilla	1 tsp.
250 mL	egg whites (7-8)	1 cup
2 mL	cream of tartar	½ tsp.

Melt 250 mL (1 cup) sugar in heavy skillet over low heat without stirring until clear and **medium** brown only. Remove from heat. Add water. Stir over low heat until lumps dissolve. Set aside.

Preheat oven to 160°C (325°F). Sift flour, sugar, baking powder and salt into mixing bowl. Make a well in centre, and add in order, the salad oil, unbeaten egg yolks, cold water, vanilla, 90 mL (6 tbsps.) burnt sugar syrup. Beat until smooth. Measure egg whites and cream of tartar into large mixing bowl. Beat until very stiff but not dry. Egg whites are stiff enough when a rubber spatula drawn through leaves a clear path. Pour egg yolk mixture **gradually** over whipped egg whites, **gently** folding with rubber scraper, just until blended.

Do not overstir. Pour immediately into ungreased 2 L (10″) tube pan. Bake in 160°C (325°F) oven for 55 minutes; then at 180°C (350°F) for 10 to 15 minutes, or until cake springs back when lightly touched. Immediately turn pan upside down, and let hang free of table until cool.

Serves 12.

62

CARROT CAKE WITH CREAMY SUPREME FROSTING

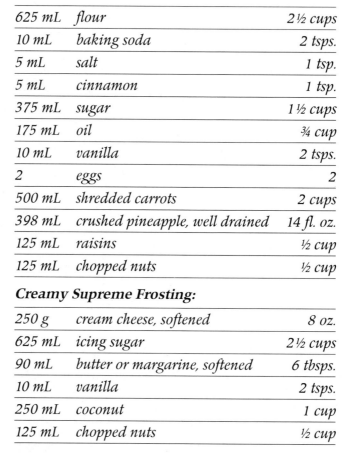

625 mL	flour	2½ cups
10 mL	baking soda	2 tsps.
5 mL	salt	1 tsp.
5 mL	cinnamon	1 tsp.
375 mL	sugar	1½ cups
175 mL	oil	¾ cup
10 mL	vanilla	2 tsps.
2	eggs	2
500 mL	shredded carrots	2 cups
398 mL	crushed pineapple, well drained	14 fl. oz.
125 mL	raisins	½ cup
125 mL	chopped nuts	½ cup

Creamy Supreme Frosting:

250 g	cream cheese, softened	8 oz.
625 mL	icing sugar	2½ cups
90 mL	butter or margarine, softened	6 tbsps.
10 mL	vanilla	2 tsps.
250 mL	coconut	1 cup
125 mL	chopped nuts	½ cup

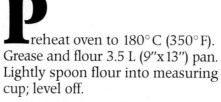

Preheat oven to 180°C (350°F). Grease and flour 3.5 L (9"x13") pan. Lightly spoon flour into measuring cup; level off.

In medium bowl, combine flour, baking soda, salt and cinnamon; set aside. In large bowl, combine sugar, oil, vanilla and eggs; beat well. Stir in flour mixture; mix well. Stir in carrots, pineapple, raisins and nuts. Pour into prepared pan. Bake 50 to 60 minutes or until cake springs back when touched lightly in center. Cool completely.

Frosting:

In medium bowl, combine cream cheese, icing sugar, margarine and vanilla; beat until smooth. Stir in coconut and nuts. Spread over cooled cake.

Makes 16 servings.

HUMMINGBIRD CAKE

750 mL	flour	3 cups
375 mL	sugar	1 ½ cups
5 mL	salt	1 tsp.
5 mL	soda	1 tsp.
5 mL	cinnamon	1 tsp.
3	eggs, beaten	3
375 mL	oil	1 ½ cups
7 mL	vanilla	1 ½ tsps.
175 mL	crushed pineapple, undrained	¾ cup
500 mL	mashed bananas	2 cups
500 mL	chopped pecans	2 cups
	Whole pecans, garnish	

Icing:

250 g	cream cheese	8 oz.
125-250 mL	brown sugar	½-1 cup
15-30 mL	milk	1-2 tbsps.

Preheat oven to 160°C (325°F). Grease and flour two 1.2 L (8") round cake pans. Combine first five dry ingredients in a large bowl. Combine eggs with oil, vanilla, crushed pineapple, bananas and 375 mL (1½ cups) of the chopped pecans in another bowl. Add wet ingredients to dry ingredients and stir until moistened throughout. Pour into prepared pans. Bake 1 hour and 15 minutes or until a toothpick comes out dry when cake is tested. Remove from oven and let cool on cake racks 10 minutes. Remove cakes from pans. Set aside to cool completely.

Make icing by creaming cream cheese with brown sugar to taste. Add 5 mL (1 tsp.) of milk at a time until icing is spreadable. Put first cake layer on cake plate and spread icing to cover top. Place next layer on top and with serrated knife trim cake to make it even. Ice cake and press remaining 125 mL (½ cup) chopped pecans onto sides. Garnish with whole pecans.

Favorite
Cookies, Squares
and Candies

WHOLE WHEAT FRUIT BARS

75 mL	shortening	⅓ cup
250 mL	packed brown sugar	1 cup
2	eggs	2
5 mL	vanilla	1 tsp.
175-300 mL	flour	¾ -1 ¼ cups
175-300 mL	whole wheat flour	¾ -1 ¼ cups
1 mL	baking soda	¼ tsp.
10 mL	baking powder	2 tsps.
5 mL	grated orange rind	1 tsp.
	pinch of salt	

Fruit Filling:

540 mL	fruit pie filling, any kind	19 oz. can

In a large bowl, beat together shortening, brown sugar, eggs and vanilla until creamy. Add both flours (using lesser amounts), baking soda, baking powder, orange rind and salt, beating until blended. Add remaining flour if dough is sticky. Refrigerate dough 1 to 2 hours.

To bake cookies preheat oven to 190° C (375° F). Grease baking sheets. On a floured surface, roll dough into a 35 cm (14") square. Cut dough into 4 equal strips, each 35 cm (14") long and 8.5 cm (3½") wide. Spoon ¼ of fruit filling in a 3.5 cm (1½") wide ribbon down the centre of each strip. Using a long spatula, lift sides of each dough strip over filling, slightly overlapping on top. Press edges together to seal. Cut strips crosswise into 2.5 cm (1") pieces. Place, seam-side down 7.5 cm (3") apart on greased baking sheet. Brush off any excess flour.

Bake 12 to 15 minutes or until puffed and firm to the touch. Cool 5 to 10 minutes on baking sheets. Lightly dust top with icing sugar and cinnamon. Remove to rack and cool completely.

Makes about 4 dozen.

CARDAMOM COOKIES

125 mL	butter or margarine	½ cup
125 mL	firmly packed brown sugar	½ cup
50 mL	light cream	¼ cup
375 mL	flour	1 ½ cups
10 mL	ground cardamom	2 tsps.
2 mL	baking soda	½ tsp.
2 mL	salt	½ tsp.

In a large bowl cream together butter and sugar until light and fluffy. Beat in cream.

Sift together flour, cardamom, baking soda and salt. Stir this mixture into butter mixture.

Chill dough for 1 hour or until it is firm enough to handle. Form dough into a 25 cm (10") roll on sheet of waxed paper. Wrap roll in waxed paper and freeze for at least 2 hours. Preheat oven to 190° C (375° F). Cut roll into 6 mm (¼") slices and arrange them on an ungreased cookie sheet. Sprinkle each slice with a pinch of sugar and bake for 6 to 8 minutes, or until edges are golden brown.

Makes 40 cookies.

CHEWY GUMDROP OATMEAL COOKIES

250 mL	sifted flour	1 cup
2 mL	baking powder	½ tsp.
2 mL	baking soda	½ tsp.
2 mL	salt	½ tsp.
125 mL	shortening	½ cup
125 mL	packed brown sugar	½ cup
125 mL	sugar	½ cup
1	egg	1
15 mL	water	1 tbsp.
5 mL	vanilla	1 tsp.
375 mL	uncooked rolled oats	1 ½ cups
175 mL	gumdrops, cut into small pieces, OR Smarties	¾ cup
375 mL	flaked coconut (optional)	1 ½ cups

Preheat oven to 180°C (350°F). Sift together flour, baking powder, soda and salt. Add shortening, sugars, egg, water, vanilla; beat until smooth. Fold in rolled oats and gumdrop pieces. Shape mixture into walnut-size balls and roll in coconut, if desired. Place on ungreased cookie sheet. Bake 12 to 15 minutes.

Makes 3-4 dozen.

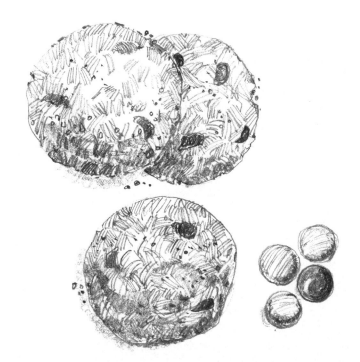

67

WALNUT THIMBLE COOKIES

Topping:

125 mL	firmly packed brown sugar	½ cup
50 mL	sour cream	¼ cup
2 mL	cinnamon	½ tsp.
250 mL	chopped walnuts or pecans	1 cup

Dough:

125 mL	butter or margarine	½ cup
250 mL	firmly packed brown sugar	1 cup
1	egg	1
5 mL	vanilla	1 tsp.
500 mL	flour	2 cups
2 mL	baking soda	½ tsp.
1 mL	salt	¼ tsp.
15-50 mL	water	1-3 tbsps.

Icing:

125 mL	icing sugar	½ cup
15 mL	water	1 tbsp.

Prepare topping: In small bowl, stir together sugar, sour cream and cinnamon until smooth. Stir in nuts, set aside.

Prepare dough: Preheat oven to 180° C (350° F). In mixer bowl cream butter and sugar. Add egg and vanilla; beat until light and fluffy. On low speed, gradually add dry ingredients, beating until just smooth. Add water, if necessary. Roll dough into 2.5 cm (1″) balls; place 7.5 cm (3″) apart on ungreased baking sheets. With a fingertip or end of mixing spoon make round depression in center of each cookie. Fill depressions with topping. Bake 15 to 20 minutes until filling is set. Transfer cookies to rack to cool.

Prepare icing: Mix sugar and water until smooth. Drizzle over cookies.

Makes 3 to 4 dozen.

PECAN DELIGHTS

Like teenie pecan pies

250 mL	unsifted flour	1 cup
125 mL	butter or margarine, softened	½ cup
125 mL	cream cheese, softened	4 oz.
1	egg	1
125 mL	firmly packed light brown sugar	½ cup
90 mL	finely chopped pecans	6 tbsps.
	dash of salt	
2 mL	vanilla extract	½ tsp.
5 mL	melted butter or margarine	1 tsp.
24	pecan halves, for garnish	24

In medium mixer bowl with electric mixer at high speed, combine first three ingredients. Roll dough with well-floured rolling pin on a well-floured board to 6 mm (¼″) thickness. Cut dough with 6 cm (2½″) cookie cutter; put in 4 cm (1¾″) tart pans. Place in freezer for 10 - 15 minutes or in refrigerator for one hour to firm. Preheat oven to 180° C (350° F).

Meanwhile, in small bowl, mix egg and remaining ingredients except pecan halves. Set aside. When firm, fill each shell with one teaspoon pecan mixture and top with an additional pecan half, if desired. Bake 30 minutes or until lightly browned. Cool completely on wire racks.

Makes 2 - 2½ dozen.

69

LEMON CURD COCONUT BARS

Coconut Base:

375 mL	sweetened flaked coconut	1½ cups
250 mL	flour	1 cup
50 mL	granulated sugar	¼ cup
125 mL	cold butter or margarine	½ cup

Lemon Curd Topping:

3	eggs	3
250 mL	sugar	1 cup
75 mL	fresh lemon juice	⅓ cup
15 mL	finely grated lemon rind	1 tbsp.
15 mL	flour	1 tbsp.
1 mL	salt	¼ tsp.

Prepare base: Preheat oven to 180°C (350°F). In a large bowl combine coconut, flour and sugar. Cut butter into small bits and add it to the mixture. Blend together until mixture resembles coarse meal. Press into a buttered square 2 L (8″x 8″) pan, and bake for 15 minutes or until it is golden brown.

Prepare topping:

In a bowl, beat eggs. Add sugar, lemon juice, lemon rind, flour, and salt. Pour this mixture over baked layer and return it to the oven for 25 minutes or until the topping is golden brown in colour. Allow square to cool and cut into 5 cm x 2.5 cm (2″x1″) pieces.

Makes 32 bars.

MATRIMONIAL CAKE

Filling:

500 mL	dates	2 cups
250 mL	boiling water	1 cup
15 mL	brown sugar	1 tbsp.
30-45 mL	lemon juice	2-3 tbsps.

Add boiling water and brown sugar to dates and cook until smooth. Add lemon juice. Cool.

Crumb Mixture:

300 mL	flour	1 ¼ cups
5 mL	soda	1 tsp.
175 mL	butter	¾ cup
125 mL	brown sugar	½ cup
300 mL	rolled oats	1 ¼ cups
	Preheat oven to 180° C (350°F)	

Sift flour and soda together. Cream butter and sugar. Add rolled oats and flour mixture and rub together. Grease a 2.5 L (9"x 9"x 2") square pan and press about ½ of the mixture into the bottom of the pan. Spread on date paste. Sprinkle rest of oatmeal mixture over dates. Bake 30-35 minutes. Cool and cut in squares.

Makes approximately 24 — 5 cm x 5 cm (2"x 2") squares.

BUTTER TART SQUARES

Base:

125 mL	brown sugar	½ cup
125 mL	butter or margarine	½ cup
500 mL	flour	2 cups

Topping:

4	eggs	4
250 mL	brown sugar	1 cup
250 mL	corn syrup	1 cup
150 mL	flour	⅔ cup
10 mL	vanilla	2 tsps.
500 mL	raisins	2 cups
150 mL	pecans, chopped (optional)	⅔ cup

Prepare base: Preheat oven to 180°C (350°F). Cream brown sugar and butter or margarine. Work in flour to make a crumb mixture. Press mixture into an ungreased 3.5 L (9″x13″) pan. Bake 10 minutes until lightly browned.

Meanwhile prepare topping: Beat eggs and sugar until thick. Continue beating and add corn syrup. Stir in flour and vanilla, then add raisins and pecans. Spread over base layer. Bake in 180°C (350°F) oven for 30 to 40 minutes or until center is almost firm. When cool cut into squares. Yield: 54 squares. (2.5 cm x 5 cm/1x 2″)

COCONUT PEAKS

50 mL	butter or margarine	¼ cup
500 mL	sifted icing sugar	2 cups
50 mL	light cream	¼ cup
750 mL	shredded coconut	3 cups
350 g	semi-sweet chocolate chips	12 oz.
10 mL	vegetable shortening	2 tsps.

In saucepan, slowly heat butter until golden brown; gradually stir in next 3 ingredients. Drop by teaspoonfuls onto waxed paper; chill until easy to handle; then shape into peaks. Melt chocolate and shortening very slowly over hot, not boiling, water. Stir until smooth. Dip bottom of each peak into chocolate; let harden on cookie sheet covered with waxed paper.

Makes 2-3 dozen.

73

CHOCOLATE REDSKINS

250 mL	semi-sweet chocolate chips	1 cup
125 mL	butterscotch chips	½ cup
5 mL	butter or margarine	1 tsp.
500 mL	salted Spanish peanuts	2 cups

Line 2 baking sheets with waxed paper. In top of double boiler over hot (not boiling) water, melt together chocolate, butterscotch chips and butter. Remove from heat; stir well with wooden spoon until smooth and uniformly blended. Add peanuts and mix until well coated with chocolate mixture.

Drop rounded spoonfuls onto waxed paper. Refrigerate until chocolate is firm. Place between layers of waxed paper in an airtight container. Store in refrigerator.

Makes 48.

TURKISH DELIGHT

125 mL	cold water	½ cup
30 mL	unflavoured gelatin	2 tbsps.
500 mL	sugar	2 cups
1 mL	salt	¼ tsp.
125 mL	boiling water	½ cup
50 mL	strained orange juice	¼ cup
30 mL	strained lemon juice	2 tbsps.
	red colouring (paste or liquid), optional	
125 mL	toasted almonds, chopped	½ cup
	icing sugar or berry sugar	

In a small bowl soften gelatin in the cold water. Combine sugar, salt and boiling water in a saucepan and bring to a boil. Add softened gelatin to hot syrup and stir until dissolved. Boil slowly for 20 mins. Skim away any scum. Add orange and lemon juices to hot mixture together with colouring, if desired. Allow to cool, and when starting to thicken, add nuts.

Pour into 20 cm x 10 cm (8"x 4") loaf pan which has been rinsed in cold water. Allow mixture to cool until thick and firm. With a wet, sharp knife, loosen around edges of pan, turn out onto a board lightly covered with icing sugar. Cut into cubes and roll in icing sugar, or berry sugar.

Makes 30 cubes.

GINGERY GINGER FUDGE

200 g	candied ginger	6 oz.
175 mL	milk	¾ cup
500 mL	sugar	2 cups
250 mL	brown sugar	1 cup
30 mL	light corn syrup	2 tbsps.
30 mL	butter	2 tbsps.
5 mL	vanilla	1 tsp.

Cut ginger in small chunks with kitchen scissors. If ginger has sugar crystals attached, soak in milk, then drain, but save milk for fudge. Cook white sugar, brown sugar, milk and corn syrup over medium heat until a little dropped in cold water forms a soft ball or candy thermometer reaches 110°C (230°F).

Dissolve any sugar crystals on sides of pan by using a pastry brush dipped in water and then brushed against insides of pan.

Remove from range, add butter and cool to lukewarm without stirring. Butter a large pan or dish.

When candy is cool, add ginger and vanilla extract. Beat until fudge begins to thicken. Pour into buttered 2 L (8"x 8") pan and mark off into squares before fudge sets completely.

Makes 32 pieces.

Happy Anniversary!

Natural gas service arrived in southern Alberta in the summer of 1912, marked by flare-lighting ceremonies July 12 in Lethbridge and July 17 in Calgary. Those are the dates on which most of Canadian Western's diamond jubilee celebrations in 1987 are based. Actually, the story of natural gas in southern Alberta started long before 1912.

Eugene Coste, considered the father of the natural gas industry in Canada, brought the first commercial discoveries in Ontario into production in 1889. The Alberta natural gas saga began when Coste travelled west to investigate the possibility of drilling for natural gas near Bow Island, between Lethbridge and Medicine Hat. Coste, then working as a consulting geological engineer with the Canadian Pacific Railway, was convinced that there was an almost unlimited amount of natural gas in the Bow Island field.

On a February day in 1909 Coste and his chief driller, W.R. "Frosty" Martin, brought in the "Old Glory" well on the bank of the South Saskatchewan River near Bow Island — and the dream began to transform into reality.

Incorporated on July 19, 1911, the Canadian Western Natural Gas, Light, Heat and Power Company Limited then proceeded to build a pipeline —

the longest of its size in North America at the time — which would bring gas to Lethbridge, Calgary, Okotoks and Nanton in 1912. That same year Canadian Western also brought service to Brooks.

And so, the Canadian Western story began! This publication is one of several special projects initiated in 1987 to celebrate this historic service milestone.

Canadian Western Natural Gas
Service since 1912

The Blue Flame Kitchen

Service Since 1929

In 1929, seventeen years after Canadian Western first brought natural gas service to southern Alberta, the company established its Home Service Department — a service that today is best-known as the Blue Flame Kitchen.

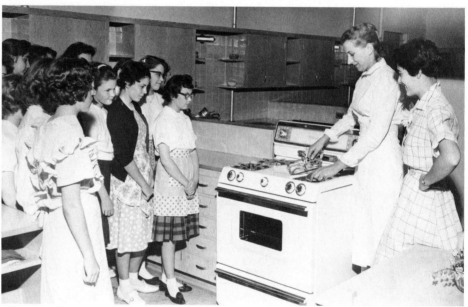

Classroom demonstration, 1958.

Radio Program, 1936.

The department — a startling development in consumer service at the time — was formed to help homemakers get the best results when using the exciting new cooking fuel, natural gas, which was quickly replacing coal as a source of energy in the home. Cooking schools and appliance demonstration classes were held throughout Canadian Western's service territory, soon becoming an

Television show, 1957.

institution in southern Alberta communities. Originally aimed solely at housewives, over the years the programs have expanded to include offerings for everyone. Recently gourmet, canning, bread making and outdoor cooking classes have been particularly popular.

Through its history the department has used new technology and means of communication to best advantage, taking its consumer information to a much wider audience through radio and television — both live and on tape. Today, responding to the day-to-day calls and letters from natural gas customers needing help with specific household problems is the backbone of the department's service to the public. Tens of thousands of calls are answered each year by the experienced staff which includes seven graduate home economists (two of whom are at Lethbridge), plus two assistants.

More than anything else, homemakers appreciate the special services the Blue Flame Kitchen provides that are not readily available from any other source. A good example of this is their thorough testing of recipes so that they are fully effective in the climates and altitudes of southern Alberta.

Testing recipes, 1983.

Calgary and Lethbridge staff of the Blue Flame Kitchen, 1987. Front row, from left: Mary Ann Joly, Donna Spronk, Loretta Vincent, Rosa Raho, Cheryl Mark, Linda West. Behind: Sharon Cummins, Evelyn Erdman and Brenda Dobson.

BLUE FLAME KITCHEN
Homemakers Service

Midnapore Christmas demonstration, 1986.

Index

BREADS

36. Sweet Dough
37. Kugelhopf
38. Jalepeno Cheese Buns
39. Pumpernickel Brie Wreath
40. Sticky Cinnamon Knots
41. Coconut Buns
42. Orange Bubble Bread
43. Crunchy Health Bread

CAKES

54. Maraschino Chocolate Cake
55. Poppy Seed Lemon Loaf
56. Spiced Pumpkin Roll
57. Date Cake
58. Raspberry Pecan Torte
59. Orange Mocha Gateau
60. Hazelnut Torte
61. Burnt Sugar Chiffon Cake
62. Carrot Cake With Creamy Supreme Frosting
63. Hummingbird Cake

COOKIES, SQUARES AND CANDIES

64. Whole Wheat Fruit Bars
65. Cardamom Cookies
66. Chewy Gumdrop Oatmeal Cookies
67. Walnut Thimble Cookies
68. Pecan Delights
69. Lemon Curd Coconut Bars
70. Matrimonial Cake
71. Butter Tart Squares
72. Coconut Peaks
73. Chocolate Redskins
74. Turkish Delight
75. Gingery Ginger Fudge

DESSERTS

44. Peach Flan
45. Frosted Meringue with Kiwis
46. Imperial Rice with Crepe Ruffles
47. Black Forest Souffle
48. Pumpkin Cheesecake
49. Raspberry Mandarin Orange Trifle
50. Canteloupe Sorbet
51. Rhubarb Cobbler
52. Apple Ring with Eggnog Sauce
53. Angel Lemon Delight

ENTREES

19. Bacon-Stuffed Trout
20. Roast Beef and Never Fail Yorkshire Pudding
21. Three Cheese Meatloaf in Puff Pastry
22. Seafood Lasagna
23. Maple Flavored Ribs
24. Stuffed Pork with Curry Sauce
25. Jambalaya
26. Honey Orange Spiced Chicken
27. Spinach-Stuffed Chicken Legs
28. Barbecued Stuffed Leg of Lamb

HORS D'OEUVRES

1. Lamb Sosaties with Fruit
2. Chinese Meatballs with Plum Sauce
3. Taco Tartlettes
4. Salmon Pate
5. Cheesy Shrimp Balls
6. Country Egg Roll Triangles
7. Spinach Dip

SOUPS AND SALADS

8. Vegetable Soup
9. Calcutta Mulligatawny Soup
10. Baked Minestrone
11. Seafood Soup
12. White Bean and Ham Soup
13. Shrimp and Cucumber Ring
14. Fruit and Cabbage Slaw
15. Orange Chicken Salad with Almonds
16. Lemon Lettuce Wedges
17. Fire and Ice Tomatoes
18. Old Fashioned Potato Salad with Boiled Salad Dressing

VEGETABLES

29. Cointreau Carrot Coins
30. Pepper Pea Pod Skillet
31. Ratatouille
32. Lemon Sweet Potatoes
33. Spanakopitta
34. Potato Pinwheels
35. Broccoli-Stuffed Potatoes

My Favorites

_____
_____
_____
_____
_____
_____
_____
_____
_____
_____
_____
_____

Notes

A Gift for all Occasions!

You can buy additional copies of 75 FAVORITES at any Canadian Western office.

If you prefer, we will mail you one or more copies.

Complete one of these coupons (save others for upcoming occasions) and mail with cheque or money order payable to:

The Blue Flame Kitchen
Canadian Western Natural Gas
909 - 11th Avenue S.W.
Calgary, Alberta
T2R 1L8

BLUE FLAME KITCHEN
Homemakers Service

The Blue Flame Kitchen
Canadian Western Natural Gas
909 - 11th Avenue S.W.
Calgary, Alberta T2R 1L8

Please send me _____ copy(ies) of 75 FAVORITES.
Enclosed is $9.95 plus $2.00 postage for each copy.

NAME _____

ADDRESS _____

_____

CITY _____ PROV. _____

POSTAL CODE _____ Allow 3 weeks for delivery.

The Blue Flame Kitchen
Canadian Western Natural Gas
909 - 11th Avenue S.W.
Calgary, Alberta T2R 1L8

Please send me _____ copy(ies) of 75 FAVORITES.
Enclosed is $9.95 plus $2.00 postage for each copy.

NAME _____

ADDRESS _____

_____

CITY _____ PROV. _____

POSTAL CODE _____ Allow 3 weeks for delivery.

The Blue Flame Kitchen
Canadian Western Natural Gas
909 - 11th Avenue S.W.
Calgary, Alberta T2R 1L8

Please send me _____ copy(ies) of 75 FAVORITES.
Enclosed is $9.95 plus $2.00 postage for each copy.

NAME _____

ADDRESS _____

_____

CITY _____ PROV. _____

POSTAL CODE _____ Allow 3 weeks for delivery.